The Two Marys

SYLVIA BROWNE

The TWO MARYS

The Hidden History of the Mother and Wife of Jesus

DUTTON

DUTTON
Published by Penguin Group (USA) Inc.
375 Hudson Street, New York, New York 10014, U.S.A.
Penguin Group (Canada), 90 Eglinton Avenue East, Suite 700, Toronto, Ontario M4P 2Y3,
Canada (a division of Pearson Penguin Canada Inc.); Penguin Books Ltd, 80 Strand, London
WC2R 0RL, England; Penguin Ireland, 25 St Stephen's Green, Dublin 2, Ireland (a division of
Penguin Books Ltd); Penguin Group (Australia), 250 Camberwell Road, Camberwell, Victoria
3124, Australia (a division of Pearson Australia Group Pty Ltd); Penguin Books India Pvt Ltd,
11 Community Centre, Panchsheel Park, New Delhi—110 017, India; Penguin Group (NZ), 67
Apollo Drive, Rosedale, North Shore 0632, New Zealand (a division of Pearson New Zealand
Ltd); Penguin Books (South Africa) (Pty) Ltd, 24 Sturdee Avenue, Rosebank, Johannesburg
2196, South Africa

Penguin Books Ltd, Registered Offices: 80 Strand, London WC2R 0RL, England

Published by Dutton, a member of Penguin Group (USA) Inc.

First printing, November 2007

1   3   5   7   9   10   8   6   4   2

 REGISTERED TRADEMARK—MARCA REGISTRADA

LIBRARY OF CONGRESS CATALOGING-IN-PUBLICATION DATA
HAS BEEN APPLIED FOR

ISBN 978-0-525-95043-1

Printed in the United States of America
Set in Goudy Old Style
Designed by Amy Hill

While the author has made every effort to provide accurate telephone numbers and Internet
addresses at the time of publication, neither the publisher nor the author assumes any
responsibility for errors, or for changes that occur after publication. Further, the publisher does
not have any control over and does not assume any responsibility for author or third-party Web
sites or their content.

To Mother God, Azna

Contents

INTRODUCTION   *XIII*

1. Powerful Women   *1*

2. The Jealousy of the Others   *33*

3. The Miracle of Human Compassion   *61*

4. History's Most Beloved Gnostics   *99*

5. The Great Pilgrimage   *123*

6. The Church That Won   *147*

7. A Woman for the Ages   *183*

APPENDIX: The Tenets of Novus Spiritus   *217*

Thank you to my staff and my grandchildren
for their love and support.

Introduction

JUST AS MUCH has been written about Jesus Christ, there have been many books written about Mary Magdalene and Mary the mother of Jesus. The phenomenal and continuing success of Dan Brown's book *The Da Vinci Code* has sparked the interest and curiosity of millions in Mary Magdalene and inspired a number of recent books about her. The books on Mary the mother of Christ are usually confined to the visions or manifestations of her in various parts of the world. This includes Bernadette at Lourdes and the three children she appeared to in Portugal in 1917. The problem with writing about both of these

Marys is the dearth of information about them. Both get lost in the New Testament of the Bible and the various religious writings of Christendom, and both were suppressed by the Catholic Church. It is only recently that the Church has recognized the true value of these women who played such an important part in the life of our Lord.

This book was written to shed some truth and illumination on these two women. They were more powerful and a greater light and support system to Jesus than anyone gives them credit for. This book emphasizes not only their relationship with each other, but also the profound influence they had in their interactions with our Lord.

In writing this book, I have melded the few known facts about these two fascinating women with the information I have received from my spirit guide Francine. I believe this will give the reader a clearer insight and more accurate picture of the truth about them. In some instances, the truth might create some controversy and ruffle the feathers of those who have believed or put forth an inaccurate picture in the name of religion, but truth always finds a way to eventually come to the foreground for all to see.

An example of this is of course the reversal of the

Catholic Church's stance on Mary Magdalene. She was at first declared a harlot and was put forth to the masses as such for hundreds of years, until the facts could no longer substantiate that viewpoint. The Church then reversed itself in 1969 and admitted it had erred, putting forth a more holy and revered outlook on Mary Magdalene.

We can also look at the various visions or manifestations of what most consider to be Mary the mother of Jesus. Francine, my spirit guide, says that all of these visions and manifestations were of the Mother God Azna and not Mary the mother of Jesus. Controversial, you say? Yes, but notice that in all of these visions and manifestations there is no mention anywhere that the woman manifesting called herself Mary. She is called the "lady" in most instances or even the "mother of god," but never names herself.

Even though both of these Marys have been misrepresented and suppressed by various factions of religion, I think you will enjoy reading about them and how much they influenced our Lord. As always, it is the truth as I know it to be.

One last bit of information before we start. In writing this book, I was amazed to find out that I actually had visions of what was happening and what was being said. This has never happened to me before, and these visions were very clear and precise. To tell the truth, I was somewhat taken aback at first, until I realized that this was a manifestation of the infusion that I was getting from God. I can also say with all humility that I knew these visions had to be communicated through my writing, and to the best of my ability, I have done just that. God does work in mysterious ways, and I felt blessed to describe these visions in these pages, which describe the lives of Jesus, Mary, and Magdalene and all of the interactions that they had together. It was like I was actually there and experienced all that was happening as they were experiencing it. I just hope I have done them justice. Now, onward to their incredible journey together.

The Two Marys

CHAPTER 1

Powerful Women

I N MY BOOK *The Mystical Life of Jesus*, I touched on the fact that in the early formative years of Christianity women taught, gave classes and knowledge, and even held what we might term "services" in honor of Jesus. This is nothing more than a continuation of ancient traditions in which children were taught at their mother's knee about religion, God, and life. As Christianity became more formalized and dogmatic in the second century of the Common Era, women were weaned out of any significant role in the "new religion." With the Council of Nicaea, held in the early fourth century and presided over by the Roman emperor Constantine, Christianity became a purely patri-archal religion, and women were completely pushed out from holding any power in the hierarchy. If the Church had been formed today, there would have been a tremendous uprising by not only feminists, but human rights groups. But history is history, and the Church was formed at a time when women were considered less than and subservient to men. What today would have stirred tremendous contro-versy was almost universally accepted at that time.

Women were not only considered inferior to men in intellect but, not to be gross, they also had menstrual peri-ods. Judaic and other ancient traditions taught that when a woman was bleeding due to her menstrual cycle, she was unclean, and many times even banished or temporarily quarantined until her cycle was over. You can't judge this too harshly because old beliefs die hard, and not having any scientific understanding of ovulation or how children are nourished in the womb helped them maintain the false idea that blood can be impure, and anyone that bleeds every month had to be less than perfect. It was in this time of male domination that both Mary Magdalene and Mary the mother of Jesus were born.

. . .

As many of us know, Mary as well as Joseph was of royal lineage, which in turn made Jesus part of their royal Davidic line. What is not known by many is that Mary Magdalene also had distant royal lineage in her family, which was considered wealthy for the time. (Author's note: For the purpose of differentiating between both of these women named Mary, Mary the mother of Christ will always be referred to as Mary and Mary Magdalene will always be referred to as Magdalene.) Both of their families were wealthy (with like associating with like), and therefore Jesus and Magdalene played together as children—even though Magdalene was about ten years younger than Christ. Francine says that many times Jesus was like a baby-sitter for Magdalene because of the age difference, but he sometimes told her (whether it was a form of teasing or just genuine affection) that when she grew up they would be married. Francine says that little Magdalene just absolutely adored Jesus when they were children and, conversely, constantly and laughingly reminded him that they would be man and wife someday. This little byplay was observed by both families so often that both just accepted the fact that Jesus and little Magdalene were betrothed from her birth.

The families of both Jesus and Magdalene were very close friends, and Magdalene was often left with Mary and Joseph because of her love for them as well as Jesus. Mary was like a second mother to Magdalene and they became very close. When Jesus left on his travels to India, Turkey, and the far reaches of the Middle East with two of his brothers and servants, Magdalene stayed with Mary more than her real family. In the fifteen years or so that Jesus was gone to learn the philosophies and teachings of other countries, Magdalene grew to five foot six, which was tall for that day and age. She had long reddish hair that flowed in massive unruly curls and was somewhat lighter in complexion than Jesus and his mother. Mary was dark haired, had a very long and oval face, and was more full figured than Magdalene. Francine says that Mary and Magdalene had magnificent eyes, like our Lord. His were so dark they almost seemed black, with golden flecks that reflected the sun in full light. Mary's were brown and had a softness about them that attracted many. Magdalene also had brown eyes but with more hazel tints, and as my guide says, they always seemed to have a flame that exuded from them. This, I'm sure, was a portent of things to come.

Neither woman was like what we might think of as the typical submissive Judaic woman. They were not held in lower esteem by their peers because of their sex, and Joseph certainly felt Mary was a powerful force and often deferred to her on all manner of business and life in general. While Magdalene was basically nurtured by Mary and Joseph in their family compound, she did manifest somewhat of a stubborn streak. She wasn't unruly, but she developed her own mind-set. Because of their wealth, both Mary and Magdalene could read and write (we'll get into that later, when we explore the Gospel of Mary Magdalene), which was rare for women at that time.

When Jesus left to travel to the Far East, Magdalene grew up and helped with the other children who were left behind. She became especially close to James (who also became an avid disciple and follower of Jesus) when he returned early after several years, having been sent home with his brother John by Jesus, to help the family. Magdalene pestered James and John a great deal for information about Jesus and their travels. James was more talkative, and he and Magdalene formed a close bond in their discussions. Even at a young age, she had a Gnostic calling and almost inhaled all the information James and John could give on the philosophies and teachings that both they and Christ had absorbed. Being very close, Mary and Magdalene would sit in the evenings and ponder where Jesus was and how life fared for him. They both began to study and talk about any and all information that James and John could give them, so that they wouldn't be left out or feel too ignorant when Jesus returned.

Of the two women, Mary was more the earth mother, and anyone in the area who needed help came to her for healing, food, and sometimes even money. Magdalene was truly a humanitarian as she got older, but was more into verbiage, writing, and teaching to feed the soul. I'm sure that this of course would have fit into our Lord's Chart perfectly—to have an intellectual counterpart in Magdalene and Mary as the sustainer. They seemed to form their own trinity of what Jesus would need in his public life and even after.

Throughout her life, Magdalene stayed closer to Jesus's

family. It's almost as if she knew that her Chart was destined to be intertwined with his. Mary was the constant mother figure but had no shyness when it came to giving advice. When asked, she was always an objective advisor. The Bible is remiss in including information on both Marys, but omits even more when it comes to Jesus's mother. After the marriage of Jesus to Magdalene at the wedding feast of Cana, she drops from sight until we pick up with her and Magdalene standing together at the crucifixion. We hear more about Magdalene in a few sequences after Jesus's supposed death on the cross. In the apocryphal Gospel of Philip there are references to the disciples being jealous of Magdalene "because Jesus seemed to favor or love her best." It's somewhat disturbing and in a perverse way comforting to see that life never changes—jealousy still rears its head.

The famous quote between Ruth and her first mother-in-law, Noemi, could be very applicable to Mary, Magdalene, and Jesus: *"For whithersoever thou shalt go, I will go: and where thou shalt dwell, I also will dwell. Thy people shall be my people, and thy God my God."* (Ruth 1:16). So in essence we are left with these shadow figures who were a backdrop of loving, active support in Christ's mission. My guide Francine says that all the lost books of the Bible were filled with these feminine figures, but given the early Church's desire to form a patriarchal church, they felt these figures had to be deleted.

Magdalene had her own lonely road to follow. Women in her day were married at thirteen or fourteen or at least by age sixteen. Here she was waiting for the man she loved for close to fifteen years, making her old to marry in any society or culture. True, she was ten to eleven years younger than Jesus, but that still made her an object of some ridicule, and she had the haunting doubt that he might not come back. Or, even more frightening for her, he would come back with another woman to take her place. As charismatic and handsome as Jesus was, he could have had his pick of any number of women. Even though there was a special tie in these three, there is a human element that is part of the human flesh, which is why Christ called out at the cross, "God, why hast thou forsaken me?" Most of us know the emotions of life can take us into all the dark corners of doubt.

Mary was always there to give solace to Magdalene and

to still any fears. She knew her son and knew that he knew he was espoused to Magdalene. So they waited and studied and took care of the children who were now almost grown and out on their own. Joseph had died by this time, which would mean he lived to be close to sixty—which at that time was ancient. In a way, though, this created an even closer bond, as it left the two women to talk, shop together, sew together, and wait for the day when Jesus would come home. Francine says Mary was pleased with Magdalene that she had grown to be not only such a beauty, but a spunky, smart, and charismatic one at that.

Their living compound had a nice open-air house that was surrounded by a whitewashed wall, and the inside was furnished with lovely handmade furniture (Joseph was an expert carpenter). There was a beautiful well surrounded by rock where they would often sit because it was shaded by many olive trees. This is where Mary and Magdalene were sitting, with Mary braiding Magdalene's hair, when Jesus came through the open gate.

They were both in awe. The boy who left was now a slender, full-grown man with dark wavy hair, beautiful skin, long slim fingers on beautiful hands, and eyes that pierced and looked straight into the soul. Mary took in a deep breath and ran toward him. Magdalene was filled with every emotion and seemed rooted to the ground, for as full of fire as she was, a sudden shyness and even apprehension came over her. Would he be sorry for leaving? Did he still love her? These doubts would soon be put to rest, for after he kissed his mother, he came toward her and embraced her. He did not, however, kiss her. This was left for the marriage and espousal period.

He began to tell them of all his journeys and what he had learned in India, Turkey, and many other places, as well as his experiences with the various nomadic tribes. He was so alive and enthused with all he had learned and experienced and how he had been infused with the light of the Holy Spirit. They talked for hours, and he related that he wanted to be immediately baptized by his cousin John the Baptist to get rid of all past negativity. He only had one life. He didn't need to have more than one because he was the divine report from God.

The baptism was only symbolic, but he wanted to see John and even start his public life. Despite what the Bible omits, Mary and Magdalene went with him and were also baptized. When he saw Jesus, John proclaimed that he was the Messiah—the one who would come after him. It was a joyful reunion for both Jesus and John, despite the fact that John didn't recognize him at first. He hadn't seen Jesus for a long time.

Jesus and Magdalene then made preparations for their wedding with Mary's help. It was to be held at Cana. In the Bible, the wedding at Cana sticks out like a sore thumb. There is no lead-up to it and no conclusion, except that when Jesus turned water into wine, it was touted as his first miracle. In addition, the Bible does not specifically indicate whose wedding it actually was. As I pointed out in my book *The Mystical Life of Jesus*, however, Judaic tradition makes it abundantly clear that Jesus was the bridegroom, because the bridegroom is responsible for providing the wine. When his mother, Mary, came to him and said matter-of-factly that the guests had no wine and then just told the servants to do what Jesus bid them to do, she was aware of the tradition and knew Jesus had to supply his guests with wine. It would also have been totally rude and unthinkable for Mary or Jesus to order the servants about at another's wedding, but this would have been natural if they were *their* servants at *his* wedding, which of course they were.

In the editing of the Bible, the Church always had ulterior motives. In this instance they wanted to tout the first miracle of Jesus, but certainly didn't want anyone to know that Jesus married Magdalene or that he was married at all. Early Church fathers thought that if Jesus was married it would somehow take away or question his divinity. After all, marriage means sex and having children, and the early Church didn't want anyone thinking that Christ was just a mere human being like the rest of us. He was the Messiah and the Divine Son of God, and that viewpoint would certainly have been challenged if anyone knew he was married. The Church removed and added to the New Testament of the Bible with the constant aim of keeping Christ's divinity intact. Without that divinity, they would have no church and no religion. Who would care if the truth was bent as long as Christ's divinity was unquestioned? With men becoming the editors, mistakes ensued, which accounts for the numerous inconsistencies in the Bible. Many passages were added (especially the Book of Matthew) to make sure that no one could doubt that Jesus was the Messiah or Savior who was prophesied in the Old Testament. These passages were there to ensure that Christ's life fulfilled those prophecies—never mind that much of the history was completely false and never happened. I pointed out many of these inconsistencies in my book *The Mystical Life of Jesus,* and some are also pointed out in this book.

We never really see Christ participating in village functions in the Bible. He was comfortable with the people but wasn't a person who especially liked parties, festivals, or weddings. I feel that the story of the wedding at Cana was left in the Bible because it was his first public miracle; though he did perform miracles and healings in other lands—especially India, where they still talk of a holy man named Jesu who came and gave prophecy and performed miracles.

As an aside, when I was writing this book, I could see many of these scenarios in front of me as clearly as any clear vision that I've ever seen. Many people may not know this, but I don't outwardly see visions that often except in haunting investigations. This time, however, I actually saw the two women and the compound as clearly as if I'd been there. I know that most of what I write is infused from God, and this seems to me to be a prime example of that infusion—which helps me to describe what is going on and give descriptions of people and events that are happening.

After the marriage, our Lord really went into his public life and ministry in Israel almost immediately. He garnered two of his disciples from his family (James and John), but most he gathered from what we might refer to as the working class. This makes sense because he wanted people who could relate to the common masses. Magdalene was always at his side, and when he traveled, Mary his mother would cook or go ahead with James and find lodging.

There were other women who traveled with them, and in the Bible's Book of Acts of the Apostles it even states that women attended to the needs of the disciples. This does not have a sexual connotation, but more one of being helpers by cooking, cleaning, washing clothes, etc. Even some of the wives of the disciples would come. You must remember Jesus only traveled a few hundred miles in total (if not less) in his public life. The Gnostic way was to gather in groups of devoted followers, and Christ certainly had Gnostic leanings. Mary would administer orders to the women and generally supervise meals and such, while Magdalene would teach the children, and Jesus would speak to the masses.

Magdalene would teach all the loving principles that Jesus taught. The evenings were the best. They would all sit around and talk about the day and where they would go next. Many of the apostles would go ahead to a village to announce the coming of the charismatic speaker named Jesus. This was like an early version of what we would say is a public relations campaign.

Many people don't realize that at the time of Jesus, there were many proclaiming to be the Messiah, a proclamation that Jesus himself never made. Many Jewish sects had radical plans to overthrow the Roman rule, and their leaders were inevitably thought to be the coming Messiah. Apollonius of Tyana was a Greek and a contemporary of Christ who performed many alleged miracles and healings. Many thought John the Baptist was the Messiah because of his preaching and baptizing. But Christ outscaled them all. John the Baptist had a huge following partly because of his charisma, but he also was much more outspoken about freeing Israel from Roman rule and had his own set of devoted disciples—several of whom went over to Jesus. It was his rash preaching that eventually led to his downfall and beheading.

Magdalene had a fiery disposition and was way ahead of her time as a liberated woman. This was due not only to her Chart that destined her to be with Jesus, but it was also a quality nourished by Mary, who was brought up in a liberal home and was then married to an older man who loved and indulged her. Jesus was a perfect match for Magdalene because he believed in the equality of women, and they would often discuss spiritual and everyday matters together as partners.

To diverge for a moment, we get glimpses of strong women in the Bible: Deborah in the Book of Judges; Esther, who saved her people; Salome, who held the reins on Herod because of his lust for her; and Bathsheba, who almost destroyed a kingdom because of David's love for her. So we get some strong tidbits that suggest that maybe these weren't the shy, hidden women that the Church portrayed them to be.

There never seems to have been a time when Mary and Magdalene were separate, even though we don't hear much about Mary and only later hear about Magdalene, whom the Church tried to make a harlot. In *The Mystical Life of Jesus* I explain how they got Magdalene confused with other Marys and the unnamed adulteress whom Christ saved from stoning. What better way to dismiss a love affair than to brand her a sinner? Mary was left out so that Jesus couldn't be labeled a mother's boy who was loved and supported by these two women. Most of the expenses of Christ's ministry were borne by Mary, Magdalene, and several other wealthy women. In that time it would have made him look soft and weak rather than the reality of Jesus caring about and elevating women to an equal status with men.

There was never a lecture or sermon that the two women missed. They were learning so they could go back and teach the other women and children. It was almost like we now have hundreds of study groups in my church, Novus Spiritus, that try to keep pure the Gnostic message we are putting forth. In the beginning, most of these study groups were headed by females, but now we have many males who are leading them as well. Each study group usually has up to twenty-five or thirty people, and they meet once a week to study and hold services in either private homes or community centers. Mary and Magdalene would do this as often as time permitted, and they were always available to teach and many times taught in tandem.

Magdalene always deferred to her mother-in-law. Remember they had many years together while Jesus was traveling in the Middle and Far East. My guide Francine says Magdalene's mother had died early and, as her father was a silk merchant, gave her to Mary and Joseph to be raised by them. Not only were they friends, but they were also of royal bloodlines. They were the logical choice for a father who was gone much of the time taking caravans to faraway cities to trade. Mary loved Magdalene as her own, here again displaying the real earth mother traits that welcomed everyone to ask for advice, to be fed, or to have a place to rest for the night.

Both Magdalene and Mary (especially Mary) were knowledgeable about herbal remedies. They also both knew how to meditate, and often did this together. They had great infusion from God and between the two of them had a high degree of telepathy and psychic knowledge and ability. These abilities were not as great as those of our Lord, but both were very capable in their own right. Magdalene had a strong ability in prophecy and Mary had a strong clairvoyance in medical knowledge and illness. Magdalene had a way of getting into the mind of a person and pulling out the pain, and Mary could visualize many ills and problems in the body of an individual. Jesus did it en masse and knew instinctively what exactly was wrong with any who were sick, while both Mary and Magdalene were not as powerful as he in healing and preferred dealing with individuals one-on-one. People would come to both of them for healing of both mind and body and some soul work, but the food for the soul was more often left for Jesus to administer. He was for the masses, and while Mary taught Jesus many things about healing, most of his knowledge of healing had been garnered from the holy men of the East and the infusion from God. Francine says that Jesus had direct contact with God and many of his healings were the direct result of following what God told him to do.

We see the influence of both Marys when Jesus said, "Physician, heal thyself." Many of the healings in the

Bible that Jesus performed were related as the casting out of "demons," but we must realize that this is an archaic term that is not to be taken literally and basically means to cure illness or sickness. Ancient civilizations believed that all illness or sickness was caused by "demons" that entered the body and made a person ill. They can run the gamut from physical illness to psychological illness. Jesus, as well as both Magdalene and Mary, believed that many illnesses were caused by past lives or negative forces around people that made them sick. All three were very aware of how important hygienic practices were (as were most in the Judaic culture), but they might not have known about germs. They did, however, know that if everything was clean, illness disappeared.

Francine says that the portion in the Book of Luke about Christ casting out seven demons from Magdalene (Luke 8:2) was just inserted by the early Christian church to again take away the influence of Magdalene, just as they tried to do this by calling her a harlot and sinful woman. All of these assertions were made not only to suppress the female in Christianity, but also to make sure that the truth about the relationship between Jesus and Magdalene would remain hidden. It worked, and even to this day many Christians believe Magdalene was sinful.

Most of the other women did the menial tasks for the disciples, but Mary and Magdalene only concentrated on Jesus. They fed him, washed him, and sewed and washed his clothes. Both made sure that the clothes Christ wore were of good quality (as is evidenced by the Roman centurions throwing lots over his robe at the crucifixion), and they would sew together, making tiny blind stitches in the finest lamb's wool for the robes he wore. They would dye the inner garments with red clay.

Both Mary and Magdalene were also beautifully dressed, although they tended to dress very conservatively, in black or white wool dresses. They shied away from bangles or ostentatious jewelry of any kind and wore long scarves to cover their heads. Magdalene was always somewhat self-conscious about the red in her hair and what she called her "unruly locks." Mary would chide her that God gave her different hair to be unique and to outshine the other women. Magdalene had great self-assurance but no ego about herself. Both women seemed to put their mission ahead of anything else, except for a few human traits, such as Magdalene being more impatient than Mary. Mary was very patient and steadfast, almost like an anchor or rock for them all. Magdalene was more of a worrier about Jesus being so obviously different from the Roman world that didn't take kindly to new ideas or anything that would take away from the Romans' power or beliefs. Mary, on the other hand, seemed to be imbued with the knowledge that God was with her son and in the end it would right itself. Mary's favorite phrase was "Only good will eventually come to good."

The love between Magdalene and Jesus was so obvious that a few of the disciples became jealous (as is evident in the apocryphal gospels of Philip and Thomas as well as in Gnostic writings like the Gospel of Mary Magdalene and the Pistis Sophia). Jesus would constantly stroke and pet her head, kiss her, or hold her hand when walking. He was also very affectionate with his mother, as my boys are with me. They kiss and hug me, send me flowers and candy on Valentine's Day, give me cards and presents on my birthday, and constantly want to go out to dinner with me. On a psychological level I feel it's because like Jesus, they had their mother with them longer than any father figure. After all, in Jesus's childhood Joseph was very old, and then he died while Jesus was off on his travels. Mary and Magdalene were also affectionate, oftentimes walking arm and arm. Both were imbued, as was Jesus, with a quiet endurance. By today's standards, however, they were young. At the start of Jesus's public life, Mary was around forty-six and Magdalene was around twenty. If you look at the royal lineage of the House of David, the genetics for living to an old age are there.

Many of the disciples had their wives and children accompanying them. Jesus would often meet with them, but not like Mary and Magdalene, who would teach the children and interact with the wives on an almost daily basis. Mary also had many friends and relatives in Galilee and Nazareth, as well as in the Jerusalem and Bethlehem areas. Many of these friends and relatives were Gnostics, and as Christ's teachings were of a Gnostic nature, they were welcomed in not only Orthodox Jewish households but also in communities like Qumran, which was strictly Essene in nature. Jesus appealed to a wide range of the Jewish community at large. Unlike many, he was able to move freely in almost any type of Jewish atmosphere, from the Orthodox to the radical to the Gnostic.

I don't want to give anyone the idea that Jesus was a groupie magnet. Mary was a sort of barometer of who was a dark- or white-souled entity, and if anyone was a bit suspicious, she would in a kind and motherly way simply tell Jesus that this person or that person could not be trusted. As Jesus became more embroiled in his mission and his popularity grew, this became less and less a factor and his preaching caught the attention of both the Jewish Sanhedrin and the Pharisees. Instead of speaking to a few, he was now speaking to large groups of people. Jesus and his words could no longer remain in obscurity as his message gained more and more popularity among the masses. This is when his enemies started to rear their heads because of greed, politics, and fear.

As the popularity of Jesus rose, so did the number of people who would listen to his message. Most theologians and scholars agree that Jesus never talked to thousands or in many instances not even hundreds. This makes sense because the working class had to work to feed and care for their families. My guide Francine says the largest crowd was several hundred, but that was a sizeable number for that time, considering the heat, population, and as stated the fact that if people didn't work they didn't get paid. So it's all relative.

I love big crowds, but I also love my salons where forty or fifty people are with me all day. It's so intimate and special. You can teach and lecture, but you also get the one-on-one. Mary and Magdalene taught to mostly women and children. They shared the tenets of their belief, such as those in the Beatitudes that Christ put forth. In my church of Novus Spiritus we also have tenets (see Appendix) that Francine says are very close to the ones that Mary and Magdalene taught. We also glorify the Beatitudes, which I have always felt really outshine even the Ten Commandments, but you have to realize that Jesus modernized them in a tribute to a loving and merciful God.

Now, never would I ever negate the miracles that Jesus performed, but the popularity of Mary and her many friends and relatives gives a little different spin on one of them—namely the miracle of the loaves of bread and fishes that fed the multitude. With new research comes new information, such as the fact that in his public life Jesus spoke before crowds that mostly numbered below one hundred people. For the time period in question this is a sizeable crowd, but it is not a multitude of thousands. Mary would send women and disciples ahead to notify her friends and relatives to bring food for the crowds that were expected to hear Jesus. That is how the few loaves and fishes became enough to feed a crowd of a hundred or less. It was like what we would call a potluck today.

Magdalene was very close to John the Baptist right up to his beheading by Herod. She would constantly warn him that he was becoming too fanatical and was courting trouble from the Judaic and Roman communities. She tried to convince him to keep a lower profile, but as we know he didn't. She was the one who brought the news to Jesus that John had been beheaded, and Jesus took it very hard and even wept. The New Testament has a way of segregating stories, but we must remember that Israel was a small nation with many small villages or towns that were quite close to one another. Everyone knew of John the Baptist, and everyone knew what the Romans and King Herod and the Sanhedrin and Pharisees thought about him. It would not have taken a genius to figure out that John would sooner or later be arrested or killed, because his teachings were a constant indictment of those who ruled. In other words, the people of Israel got news fairly quickly, and it was an atmosphere of almost everyone knowing everybody else and getting the latest news even without television or newspapers.

Many people think Jesus was illiterate because he didn't go to a formal school. Because his family was fairly wealthy, he had tutors who schooled him in many languages such as his native Aramaic, as well as Greek, Hebrew, and Latin. He also frequently went to the local synagogue to learn the laws and tenets of the Judaic faith. In other words, as was the case with most of the wealthy families in Israel at the time, Jesus was given an extensive education. This served him well later on when he left home and traveled to several Middle and Far Eastern countries and he also learned the languages and different dialects spoken in Turkey, Persia, and India. Francine says he was a good pupil and often became an ardent student when he was studying subjects that interested him. Mary and Magdalene also were literate in Aramaic and did know some Latin and Greek.

Many scholars wondered why Jesus didn't write. He did

write extensively, however, Francine says his works are either yet to be found, hidden away to serve some secret or private agenda, attributed to another writer, or have been destroyed by time and ignorance. Many took notes of his travels and sermons, such as Magdalene, several of his disciples, and his brother James.

Even though Magdalene was married to Jesus, during his public life they had little alone time. Now, not for one minute would I put myself even near our Lord's position, but I know that when I'm lecturing, writing, doing readings, teaching, and traveling, there isn't much time for togetherness, and my failed marriages show that. Unlike some, however, Magdalene knew this was her journey, as Jesus's mother did. Besides, both Mary and Magdalene had each other and felt a sense of pride that they could bring about the preordained word from the Messiah.

Take note that Jesus never publicly professed that he was the Messiah except for his talk with the Samaritan woman at Jacob's well (John 4:25–26): *"The woman saith to him: I know that the Messias cometh (who is called Christ); therefore, when he is come, he will tell us all things. Jesus saith to her: I am he, who am speaking with thee."* Both Mary and

Magdalene, however, especially Magdalene, had no problem professing to everyone that he was the Christ who was the one anointed by God. But consider this: God made everything in duality, so could not Magdalene also have been anointed by God to help fulfill Christ's mission? As we will see, could she not have been anointed for her continued mission after Jesus died of old age in France?

Jesus shared his theological ideas with both Mary and Magdalene, but with Magdalene he shared his fears (after all the human part was there), his dreams, and his ideas for the future. She never betrayed his confidence. Even though they had time together in France, she knew she would outlive him. She also knew, however, that she had to carry the torch after he was gone. Conveniently, the Church ruled her out as having that role and opted for Paul—who was not a champion of women, so he fit perfectly into the patriarchal regime.

Logically, wouldn't you want to hear from the mouth of the women or woman who shared his life rather than someone who never met him and put his own spin on things he never knew? With new discoveries like the ones at Nag Hammadi and Qumran and new archaeological finds, let's all pray to God that Paul recedes and truer words come forward.

Magdalene was the chosen mate and companion for Jesus; everyone knew it, and Mary encouraged it. When Magdalene faltered, the earth mother Mary would bolster her up, saying much that I find to be logical: "What better person to help and support my son than a mate who has lived every moment with him?"

Francine said that from a very early time (approximately halfway through his ministry) Jesus was aware that he had to face a terrible trial of life. We see this at Gethsemane when he asks God to take this chalice of pain from him, and God more or less answers, "No, you wrote it and were destined for it, so you have to fulfill your mission." Magdalene and his mother were made aware of this, and it was at this point when they changed roles for a brief time. Mary, being the mother, with a mother's heart, became very worried. Magdalene then went into the "motherly" position of telling her or consoling her that it wasn't going to be pleasant, but that Jesus would survive and they could look forward to a better life.

I guess maybe it's because I'm a mother, but even

though someone consoles you, you still let your mind go everywhere. What if he dies? What if plans go awry? How can it be that someone who tries to do good and love God can be so badly treated by the world? Again, not ever putting myself anywhere near Jesus, I've seen and experienced this from the atheistic skeptics who try to defame God, the pope, religion, and especially me. I'm tough, but it's easy to feel crucified by the biased press. Good in this world has a hard road, but it is a blessed one, and whenever and wherever good rises, darkness rises to try and stop it.

CHAPTER 2

The Jealousy of the Others

THE *DA VINCI CODE* and many other books have tried and done an excellent job of surmising infor-mation on Magdalene, but there aren't many that give any information about Mary. After she was chosen by God and gave birth to Jesus, she seems to have been swept under the religious carpet, as she is mentioned only in several other scenarios in the four canonical gospels of the New Testament: finding Christ in the Temple at age twelve, the marriage at Cana, and at the crucifixion.

Even though Mary is venerated by most of Christian-ity and considered to be the most worthy of all saints, her sainthood came about through what the Church calls vox populi, or popular sentiment. In other words, the masses of early Christians venerated her so strongly that she was considered to be a saint and was incorporated as a saint by the Church before saint canonization was even put into Church doctrine. The first guidelines concerning canonization of saints were not put forth until the late tenth century in the Catholic Church and have been modified several times since. Both Mary and Magdalene were considered saints by the people long before the tenth century, as were many others, and as such were accepted by the Church without canonization. Later, the Church reviewed all of the saints made by vox populi and eliminated some of them as not worthy—the most famous being St. Christopher (who was dropped because the Church felt he was a fictional legend and not a real person).

There are Protestant sects of Christianity that believe that the veneration of Mary is wrong because it takes away from the worship of Jesus and God, and some even link it to idol worship, but that is really more of a schism between the Protestants and Catholics than an indictment of Mary. In truth, the Catholic Church was very slow in its recognition of Mary. It wasn't until 1950 that the assumption of Mary was formally declared to be dogma by the Church. In the early Church there was a lot of infighting from different factions regarding Mary; some doubted she was a virgin and others said she was a virgin for her whole life. This ran in direct parallel to the debates as to whether Jesus was indeed God incarnate or a divine messenger from God. When all the dust settled from the endless debates, it was put forth that Jesus was indeed God incarnate and was recognized as such. With this recognition of the status of Jesus, Mary was then dealt with accordingly and was named "Theotokos"—translated as either "Mother of God" or "Godbearer." This all took place at the Third Ecumenical Council held at Ephesus in 431 C.E. Over the years, her veneration by Catholics has mainly been one of intercession, using prayers to her to intercede for whatever one needed from Jesus and/or God.

As stated earlier, Magdalene was downplayed and actually named a sinner by the Church until 1969, when the Church reversed its position on her. Being the first person to see and talk to the resurrected Jesus, she had an ardent following among early Christians, who venerated her. With the advent of questions and theories brought forth by a recent deluge of books, a renewed interest in Magdalene and her part in the life of Jesus has created a new surge of popularity concerning her life. Although she has been officially cleared of any wrongdoing that had been attributed to her, most Christians today still have the image of Magdalene being either a harlot or sinner. She of course was neither.

No one has to date found any writings attributed to Mary, and perhaps future archaeological discoveries will find some. There have been writings that refer to her that are not in the New Testament and are considered more Gnostic or apocryphal in nature. The Gospel of Mary that was recently found has been attributed to Magdalene. In fact, there are portions of three different copies—two in Greek and one in the Coptic language—that have been found in the last one hundred years.

Before we go any further, I would like you to get some background information on the Gospel of Mary (Magdalene). In 1896, Dr. Carl Reinhardt purchased an ancient papyrus book in Cairo, which contained four manuscripts. He brought them to Berlin to be studied. The book was a fifth-century C.E. papyrus codex written in the Coptic language that was used by early Christians in Egypt, and it contained four works that up to that time were completely unknown: the Apocryphon of John, the Sophia of Jesus Christ, the Act of Peter, and the Gospel of Mary. This small and seemingly innocuous purchase would become one of great significance. For years Dr. Reinhardt and others studied these manuscripts, and because of bad luck and two world wars their findings were not published until 1955. By that time, both the Nag Hammadi Gnostic writings (1945) and the Dead Sea Scrolls (1947) had been discovered, and the Nag Hammadi writings contained copies written in Greek of all four of the manuscripts found in Dr. Reinhardt's book. Scholars have since named these manuscripts the Berlin Codex.

Importantly, the Codex preserves the most complete surviving copy of the Gospel of Mary (as the text is named in the manuscript, although it is clear this person named Mary is the Magdala). This can be partly found under Papyrus Berolinensis 8502. The other fragment of the Gospel of Mary, which was also written in Greek, was found at Oxyrhynchus in northern Egypt in 1917. The Berlin

Codex has the most pages of any of the three existing copies, but even at that fewer than eight pages remain of what researchers consider to be a gospel that was at least twice as long. No complete copy of this gospel has been found or is known to exist, so what we have is less than half of what the original is thought to have been. The other two fragments of the gospel found at Nag Hammadi and Oxyrhynchus are even smaller fragments, and both duplicate sections of the Berlin Codex, even though they are thought to be older (third-century Greek copies). The Coptic copy in the Berlin Codex dates from the fifth century.

As fragmentary as the Gospel of Mary is, it has still stirred a lot of controversy and has brought some new insights into our views of the apostles, the teachings of Jesus, and of course Mary Magdalene. A new outlook on Magdalene has emerged from these tiny fragments to the point where in some theologian's minds she has become "the apostle to the apostles" or even the apostle who understood the teachings of Jesus the best. From this fragment we find Magdalene teaching the apostles what Christ's teachings were about, because they didn't understand them. Our whole concept and outlook on history can be changed out of such seemingly small discoveries, for in this brief and fragmentary gospel we also read about Magdalene encouraging the fearful apostles to not be afraid and to go out into the world with Christ's message. It makes one think—if Magdalene wasn't there, would the message of Jesus have ever been brought to the world?

Some can't differentiate between Mary and the Mother God. This is perhaps due to the fact that the Catholic Church often called Mary the Mother of God, implying that Mary was the human mother to Jesus. Indeed she was, but she is not Azna the Mother God, and all of the Marian visions attributed to Mary were in actuality visions of Azna. Francine says that Mary is as adored on the Other Side as she was here. She also says that the disciples took to her better than to Magdalene, possibly because she didn't seem like a threat and was very silent in public about her feelings or ideas.

Magdalene, on the other hand, wanted to explore what Jesus said in depth and wanted to discover all the meanings behind the parables. This is what a student does, though, and strangely the other disciples didn't go to great lengths to understand what our Lord was saying. But then, they were far more afraid than she was and at times had doubts. Both Mary and Magdalene were unwavering in their knowledge of Christ's mission in life, and his life was their life. Magdalene, specifically in her later-life gospel, eliminates gender as a qualification for living a spiritual life. She always imparted that we are all just souls raising or ascending to perfection through the love of an all-loving God. Like Jesus, both Mary and Magdalene were vehement about bringing about "the new law"—not a vengeful, wrathful God, but an all-loving Entity. We, like God, should follow these simple and let's say kind and workable rules of spirituality without fear of retribution and hellfire.

Public interest about the life of Jesus and those around him has risen dramatically since the publication of the Gospel of Mary as well as the writings of Nag Hammadi and the Dead Sea Scrolls. It really started to rise when the bestselling book *Holy Blood, Holy Grail* was published in the 1980s and spurred an interest in not only Magdalene, but also in the question of whether or not Christ was married and had children.

In one of the earliest commentaries on the Song of

Songs, Hippolytus referred to Magdalene as "apostle to the apostles" in the third century (obviously before the Council of Nicaea). He did this based on not just the Gnostic accounts, but on what he researched and found her role to be. He found her to be in a higher place in Jesus's life than anyone had thought or paid attention to. He based a lot of this on the resurrection. He was very entranced with the role she played in the resurrection. Periodically, despite the bad reputation that dogged her, she kept coming forward and being remembered in her role as an apostle. Many Gnostics and early Christians believed that she received the commission to teach the male apostles how to spread the word about Jesus and his mission of love. The Church removed her and put Peter in her place, feeling that a male would carry more power than a woman. But Jesus was the one who lived with her, loved her, and gave her all his ideas and teachings to spread to the disciples and teach the world.

We must constantly remember that the early Church was created in a society in which women in general were never looked upon as equal to men. Their primary function at that time was to cook and bear children and do menial household chores. They did not vote, did not hold office in government, and were largely subservient to their husbands. Many countries didn't allow women to own property, which was the reason why so many men wanted male heirs.

Mary, on the other hand, was not privy to the information that Christ imparted to Magdalene until she heard it in Magdalene's teachings. She always gave support to her, as Magdalene was the one whom she loved, and she knew how much her son loved her. I don't ever want to give you the impression that Mary was just an add-on. Francine says that at one time (even though I'm getting ahead of myself), Magdalene was teaching the apostles and Peter began to chide her. Francine then says that Mary, like a beautiful avenging angel, went into protection mode and told them that what her son wanted to be imparted was given to Magdalene and if they honored and loved him then she must be honored also—that she carried the flame of truth and must be respected. They, like Magdalene, had known Mary all their lives and respected Mary; so they tried to be more kind even if they didn't like the fact that Magdalene had so much knowledge. They wanted her to stay more as a type of secretary rather than a mouthpiece for Jesus. But remember, she had many years with him, so this made her even more knowledgeable and in the driver's seat so to speak.

When Mary and Magdalene traveled in the three years of Jesus's public life, Magdalene did take notes, and what she didn't take was filled in and edited by Mary, who had a phenomenal memory. They were really kindred souls, best friends, and partners in a spiritual message and mission.

Jesus's favorite saying that he would often say to the women was "He who has ears to hear let him hear" (this was taken from the Gospel according to Mary Magdalene). This was also the phrase that haunted Magdalene throughout her life. She wanted the world to hear. His mother, who always had a psychic sense, kept telling Magdalene when she got discouraged that Jesus's words would eventually resound around the world. You must also remember that their world was very small compared to what we know today. The world was "flat" and basically was confined to the Roman Empire with a few other countries thrown in.

We must also understand—and it should give us great

hope no matter how down we feel—that in their divinity these women as well as Jesus were still in human form. That brought about a human side of fear, a sense of rejection, and even a desire for wanting to succeed in a tiny hamlet of the world that sometimes had to feel overwhelming. Nothing is ever accomplished without dedication, doubts, and fear of failure.

Yet Mary, Magdalene, and Jesus had their own trials cut out for them. Jesus went through a crucifixion and almost died, Magdalene persevered through the jealousy of the other apostles and the worries of a wife for her husband, and Mary suffered the worries of a loving mother for her son. They were not only bucking the known religions of the day, but later would have to leave their country and home behind to keep Jesus and his words alive and well. To make matters worse, they also had to fight the egos of some of the apostles, especially Peter, who felt that he was chosen to lead and cajole almost all of them to go out into the world and preach the word, because they were all afraid of what the Judaic and Roman powers would do to them. Unlike what the Bible tries to portray, almost all of the apostles were very reluctant and fearful for their lives.

They were not filled with such religious zeal that they happily sped off to other lands to spread Christ's ministry. We know this not only because it is in such writings as the Gospel of Mary, but also because the Bible gives large hints about their mind-set with such instances as Peter denying Christ three times and the apostles' conspicuous absence at Christ's crucifixion. They all had doubts and, being human, were very fearful that they would end up on the cross like Jesus.

Jesus constantly told his disciples to always respect and love and care for his women because they would be the messengers after his death. At the various times that he said this, he knew he would have to go through his trial and crucifixion and fully expected to die. It was only later on, near the time when this was going to take place, that one of his most ardent and faithful followers, whom I consider to be one of the greatest unsung heroes, came up with a plan to possibly have Christ survive his crucifixion. That follower was Joseph of Arimathaea. I have put this plan and all that it entailed in my book *The Mystical Life of Jesus* and will only give a brief summary here.

Joseph had a high position in the Roman government

because of his vast tin mines in the British Isles. As such, he knew many influential people, including having a close relationship with Pontius Pilate. He outlined a plan to Jesus that would not save him from being crucified but, if everything went well, could possibly save his life. Initially Joseph told Jesus that he had already bribed Pilate to save Jesus. Jesus told Joseph that part of his mission was to be crucified, his death was imminent, and that Pilate would have to condemn him. Joseph went back to Pilate and related what Jesus had told him. Interestingly, Pilate quickly came up with a revised plan that would allow Jesus to fulfill his prophecy of being crucified, but would also allow Jesus to survive. It was risky and everything had to go well for it to succeed, but Joseph convinced Jesus to at least give it a try. Jesus, being human, was somewhat dubious about its success and fully expected to die on the cross. He also, however, wanted to live if it was possible and raise a family. He reluctantly agreed. The plan, the success of which fully hinged on Pilate and the resources of Joseph of Arimathaea, was put into motion.

Pilate had met with Joseph, Jesus, and Judas—all principals in the plan and important for its success—and outlined his plan carefully to them all. Pilate was to try to save Jesus, if at all possible, from any punishment. Failing that, Pilate was to try to delay the standard punishment (flogging and crucifixion) as long as possible on the day before the Sabbath (Jewish law forbade any crucifixions on the Sabbath and also forbade any bodies being left on the cross on the Sabbath). This was to ensure that Jesus would be on the cross for the least amount of time possible, giving him the best chance at survival. Lastly, Pilate told his soldiers that this man was not to die, and consequently the flogging they gave him was minimal. The soldiers who nailed him to the cross made sure that no arteries were pierced, gave him a footrest so that he could breathe, and did not break his legs.

This was done because crucifixion is normally a process of suffocation that takes several days to kill the victim unless they break his legs. With broken legs he cannot push himself up to breathe and usually dies in six to twelve hours. Normal crucifixion victims died of suffocation after a time of several days. This happened because, without food or water and with exposure to the elements, they became too exhausted to push themselves up to breathe.

The remaining facts ensured that Christ survived. He was only on the cross for about three hours and therefore didn't suffocate. He was given an opiate to ease his pain (the sponge filled with what was supposed to be vinegar), which eventually caused unconsciousness and allowed him to feign death. He was barely pierced with a spear in his side and did not bleed enough to die. He was quickly taken off the cross at sundown, per Jewish law, and was quickly hid away in an aboveground tomb that Joseph of Arimathaea had provided. In this tomb, they could tend to his wounds and ensure his survival. Thus, this became one of the greatest and most successful plans for escaping death ever implemented. All but the few involved were none the wiser.

Now, many of you may say that this is a complete fabrication of the facts; but many facts support the premise that Jesus survived his crucifixion. Not only do you have the above facts about how long it takes to die from crucifixion, disproving the lethality of the three hours the Bible says Jesus spent on the cross, but you also have a number of other biblical portrayals that support his survival. First of all, you have the missing body from the tomb (his supposed resurrection to heaven) and the two angels asking Magdalene why she seeks the *living* among the dead. Then you have Magdalene asking a gardener (who is really Jesus in disguise whom she doesn't recognize) if he has seen our Lord. Only when he speaks does she realize he is Jesus, her adored husband. Why would he be in disguise if not to hide himself from those who would recognize him? He would only do this if he were still alive and afraid that he would be recognized, and would have no need for disguise if he were dead. When Mary tries to embrace him, he says not to touch him because his wounds are still sensitive, not because he is not of this world. This is evidenced later on when he meets with his disciples several times. In both meetings he declares to his disciples that he is alive and not of the spirit and even displays his healing wounds to convince them. The gist of this is that most people believe that Jesus met his disciples in his glorified body after the resurrection. If that was the case, why did he still have his wounds and declare that he was alive and not of the spirit? The portions of the Bible that relate these meetings with his disciples after his supposed death are the most convincing evidence of his survival. No body in spirit form carries wounds, and more than once, Jesus tells his disciples that he is indeed alive!

Francine says that Jesus helped to prepare his disciples to go out into the world to spread his teachings, but he also told them that he was going to heaven so that he could cover his escape. Now, some of you might say that this was a falsehood, but you must realize that Christ knew everyone ascended into heaven (except dark-souled entities) at their death and that he would someday die and also ascend to the Other Side. Francine says that Jesus went to Qumran (the main base of the Gnostic Essene sect) to hide until travel arrangements out of the country were finalized. One of the nicknames of Qumran was "heaven," and I think that the disciples or storytellers got their wires crossed and confused Christ's reference to the heaven that was Qumran for the heaven where all of us will eventually go. We get a hint of this at the end of the Book of John, for in John 21:25 it says, *"But there are also many other things which Jesus did; which, if they were written every one, the world itself, I think, would not be able to contain the books that should be written."* This passage to me could very well refer to the additional works that Jesus did after his escape from Israel.

Magdalene was the first to see Jesus after Joseph of Arimathaea and a few helpers had revived him and carried him away to a safe place. In the interim period he donned a disguise and insisted—despite his wounds—to meet with Magdalene and his mother as soon as possible so that they would know he was alive. Of all the things that Mary and Magdalene knew, they didn't know the intricacies of the plan to save Jesus. Jesus had only told Magdalene that there was a plan to try to save him, but to not get her hopes up. He fully expected the plan not to succeed and that he would die on the cross. He was afraid, because if anything went wrong both Magdalene and Mary would be even more devastated. He told Magdalene not to tell his mother about the plan. Of course Judas knew it because he was in on it and had to portray the role of betrayer. Mary, not being the eloquent teacher that Magdalene was, still had a tremendous intuitive ability and knew something was in the air. This was not just out of motherly love or denial; she always had a sense of what was to come. She and her son would take walks together and she would listen and also counsel him. Francine says that because she knew in her heart that her son was not going to die, she cornered Judas with that knowledge. He confided the plan to her, swearing her to secrecy. Thus, both Jesus and Magdalene thought that Mary was unaware of the plan, when in actuality she knew more of the plan than Magdalene.

While Jesus and Magdalene were meeting with his disciples after his supposed death, it was Mary who made the arrangements with Joseph of Arimathaea and Levi the disciple for their escape. Most of the people in Israel knew very little about the rest of the world, but Mary had listened to her son relate all of the wonders that lay beyond the borders of their little country. They arranged overland travel from Qumran to the seaport city of Tyre, where they boarded a boat and sailed to what is now known as Turkey. This was the first phase of a long journey that would eventually end in France, as we will see later.

I am constantly amazed at how organized religions edit out human emotions in the writings that they accept as gospel. For example, the four canonical gospels really don't mention the emotions of those who were around

Jesus that much. Oh, we see Peter denying Christ three times and the betrayal of Christ by Judas; but we really don't get much insight into the main characters who surrounded Jesus—namely Magdalene, Mary, and his twelve disciples. If we confined our viewpoint about these individuals to only what we read in the Bible, we would have a very sketchy and mostly inaccurate picture of what these people were like (example: Magdalene being viewed for two thousand years as a sinner). Thankfully, for those of us who are searching for answers, humankind has made certain discoveries in the last century or so. These include apocryphal and Gnostic writings containing other gospels that are attributed to disciples besides Matthew, Luke, Mark, and John. These writings are significant in that they not only give us more insight into our Lord and his mission, but several of them give us more insight into the people that surrounded him in his public life—especially Mary and Magdalene.

I briefly touched on the "problem" with Magdalene and Peter earlier, but would like to explore it a little further. This problem gives us more insight into the individual makeup of the people involved and also allows us to perceive more of what they were really like as human beings. The Gospel of Thomas, the Gospel of Philip, the Pistis Sophia, and the Gospel of the Egyptians all have sections within them that relate to Magdalene and her relationship with the other disciples. Peter Kirby has a good website (www.earlychristianwritings.com) that gives us some great information on early writings dealing with Christianity and the varying viewpoints of various scholars on these writings. In the section entitled "Gospel of Mary," Kirby puts forth that the noted author Karen L. King (Winn professor of ecclesiastical history at Harvard University Divinity School) had these observations in her introduction to the book *The Nag Hammadi Library*:

> The confrontation of Mary with Peter, a scenario also found in *The Gospel of Thomas, Pistis Sophia,* and *The Gospel of the Egyptians,* reflects some of the tensions in second-century Christianity. Peter and Andrew represent orthodox positions that deny the validity of esoteric revelation and reject the authority of women to teach. *The Gospel of Mary* attacks both of these positions head-on through its portray-

al of Mary Magdalene. She is the Savior's beloved, possessed of knowledge and teaching superior to that of the public apostolic tradition. Her superiority is based on vision and private revelation and is demonstrated in her capacity to strengthen the wavering disciples and turn them toward the Good.

We find that Magdalene not only possessed knowledge from Jesus that the other disciples did not have, but as is evident in these writings, she understood his teachings better than any of them. Furthermore, she taught the disciples this knowledge when called upon to do so. In all of the above writings we either get hints or actual instances when one or more of the male disciples displays jealousy toward Magdalene and comes into conflict with her either over the content of her teachings or in just the fact that she is a female and teaching them. In one or more of the above writings we also read that Jesus loved her above all of the women and/or disciples.

Now, some of these differences between the male disciples and Magdalene might just be differences of education. Magdalene's family and Joseph and Mary had her educated because they could afford the tutors needed. Peter and several other disciples were simple fishermen and in all likelihood had limited educations. How often in the accepted gospels contained in the Bible do we run across instances where the twelve disciples did not understand Christ's meaning? If you have read the Bible, you know there are certainly more than a few instances in which this happened. There were several disciples who we can assume had some education, like Matthew (also referred to as Levi), who was a publican, or tax collector, and James, who was Christ's brother; but the bulk of them seemed to have little or no education. One can envision a frustrated Jesus trying to get his teaching across to some of these uneducated disciples, which explains why he utilized parables so many times.

Regardless of educational differences, it seems Magdalene was the brightest of those around Jesus and understood his teachings better than any of them. This is one reason why she has been called by many historians and researchers the "first apostle" and "apostle to the apostles." It also may be one of the reasons why some apostles were so jealous of her. Francine says Magdalene had a highly inquisitive mind, and when she and Jesus were alone, she would pepper him with questions and receive the answers. She says Jesus loved her mind and often smiled inwardly to himself at her spunkiness. His love for her was great, but he also always had his "Father's work" paramount in his mind and soul—no doubt due to his direct contact with our Creator. Even after his public life was complete, Jesus continued to teach and prepare his apostles to go out into the world until he had to leave. If he was in Qumran in hiding, he would send Magdalene with Mary to teach them according to his instructions. Mary and Magdalene had to strengthen the resolve of the disciples and turn them toward Christ's teachings more than once. They certainly had to reinforce his message of an all-loving, merciful, forgiving, and caring God. Jesus explained to Magdalene the nature of prophecy and the rise of the soul to spirituality as its final reward. He taught her how important it was to win the battle against the wicked and illegitimate powers that seek to keep the soul entrapped in a world ignorant of its simple and truly spiritual nature. Armed with the knowledge given to her by Jesus, she tried to impart it to the disciples.

In the Gospel of Mary, Peter admonishes Magdalene because he cannot believe that a mere woman could master such elevated teaching. Andrew joins in and criticizes Magdalene, saying that her teachings do not sound like the teachings of Jesus. Magdalene begins to cry from their attack, and seeing this, Mary intervenes and pushes Levi (Matthew) to defend her. Levi does so by pointing out to Peter that he is a known hothead and is treating Magdalene as the enemy instead of her being an emissary. "We should be ashamed of ourselves," he admonishes, and says the knowledge she was given by Jesus was for their benefit. They should respect it as such and just go out and preach to the world. Later on, Jesus also admonishes them regarding Magdalene, especially when they complain that he loves her more than them (Gospel of Philip). He also admonishes them for being cowardly and in fear that the same fate that befell him will befall them. He more or less tells them to either spread the word or go about their own lives. Thus they were penitent and went out to preach. You must realize that part of the bargain with Pilate to let Jesus live was that he would not ever be a visible power again. So with his mother Mary's urging, he knew that Magdalene, who knew and loved him best, would be his mouthpiece following his so-called death.

It's interesting to note that everyone is looking for the golden chalice or Holy Grail when it was Magdalene with her fertile womb and her knowledge all along. It was while she and Jesus were hiding in Qumran that she became pregnant with their first child. Mary became a protector of Magdalene. Even though she was getting older, she still had energy, health, and beautiful skin. She was a little slower in old age, but it would be years before she had to be carried on a litter. Even then, she never lost her second sight or her mental acuity.

Think of the strength these women had to have in an all-male world. We women still face a glass ceiling, but every now and then you will see a few women that history has not risen up against despite the patriarchal hierarchy. I have never advocated a purely matriarchal spirituality, but instead a divine duality that God has manifested in all nature. Why should we negate our spiritual beliefs just because they have been slanted by the male population? I would have fought the same way if our spiritual beliefs had been purely matriarchal.

There is no doubt that Jesus is the arrow that pierces ignorance, but the full impact of the arrow does not hit the mark without the shaft and the feathers that help to carry it to its target.

CHAPTER 3

The Miracle of
Human Compassion

I WAS WATCHING THE *Today* show and there was a priest who had written about spirituality who was talking to Meredith (a cohost of the show). He stated that he thought Jesus's words were so simple, and spirituality could be summed up by the words "love your neighbor and love God." I sat there and said to myself, "Hallelujah." After fifty-four years of fighting, maybe others are getting it. That means that not only do Mary and Magdalene take their proper place, but all the dogma centered on fear and damnation—with God's help—will cease to exist. At the very least, it will be in the minority. When my ministers saw the Oprah show called "The Secret," where they were espousing that "thoughts are things" and "spirituality is simple," they didn't scream "We always knew all of this." Instead, they were elated that it's now getting into the mainstream. Who cares who hits the home run as long as the team wins? Perhaps sayings like the one Jesus spoke in the Gospel of Mary will now be respected: "He who has a mind to understand, let him understand."

Certainly, Mary's strength came from God, but it also came from seeing poverty and uprisings. She saw small Jewish uprisings in Galilee when Jesus was six to eight years old, and the Romans were not kind to those who rose against them. We see this later in the large Jewish uprising in 66 C.E. when the Temple in Jerusalem and even whole towns were leveled to the ground. The Romans took everyone they didn't kill as slaves and took all their assets. Mary could do little about the poor except help where she could, but with her deepest knowledge knew she had a son who was destined for greatness. So like many she kept a low profile and trusted in God to protect her son until his time came upon him.

When you look at this geographical area, it has always been in turmoil, whether it was occupied by some foreign power or in a state of war. The Judaic people were ruled by other nations for so many years in their history and thus have always been in fear of being annihilated. At the time of Jesus it was Rome, and now it's the time of terrorism and of Israel being surrounded by many countries that want to see the nation's demise. Sadly, the Judaic people have always had political or religious conflicts. And yet, what better place for a Messiah to originate than what was known as the Axis Mundi (center) of the known world?

Mary has always been depicted as a poor peasant woman who carried jugs of water and talked with the women at the communal well. If you go back to not just her lineage, but to the lineage and status of her husband Joseph, you'll see how erroneous this is. They had royal blood, were fairly wealthy for the time, and were respected by all. Jesus was recognized as a child of importance or he wouldn't have been presented at the Temple at birth or allowed to teach to the elders and rabbis in the Holy Temple. If he had not been from a prominent family, they would have thrown him out as an upstart child.

As we have seen, Mary was definitely a great humanitarian and not much seemed to ruffle her feathers. She was strong and had a positive outlook. Magdalene was more intense in her personality. She loved learning and teaching, but was more of a worrier and full of emotional fervor. The two of them complemented each other, which explains their close relationship.

Interestingly enough, the Islamic religion respects Mary, as it does Jesus. The faith of Islam believes Mary was visited by an angel, had a virgin birth, and produced a great messenger in Jesus—although they say there have been many messengers, which I agree with. I am Christian, but respect their beliefs and applaud the fact that they acknowledge Mary as a good force in religious history.

Mary never suffered from a bad reputation in the Bible or the Church like Magdalene did. Some religious scholars believe, however, that Mary was pregnant before she married Joseph. This caused some scandal and debate in the early Church, as some thought she had sexual relations before marriage. This was drowned out by those who put forth the virgin birth. Mary has always been revered by the general populace of Christianity and especially the Catholic Church, but as I stated earlier her assumption was not recognized until 1950. Mary made a comeback in popularity when the Church named 1954 as a Marian Year, and that year I even won a national contest for my essay about Mary.

A large amount of research has been done on Mary and Magdalene and is still ongoing, but the research on Mary is not nearly as convoluted as that done on Magdalene. There are at least four Marys that weave through the Bible, so it's no wonder it has become so confusing to everyone. On the other hand, this made it easier for the Church to portray Magdalene as the sinner and harlot who Christ saved from stoning. The fact that Magdalene was neither of these women has finally come out, and more and more research is indicating that Jesus took Magdalene as his wife and that she was raised by Mary. I'm sure that as more discoveries are made this truth will come forth, as most researchers take the position at the present time that there is no incontrovertible proof that Jesus married Magdalene.

I take the position that there is certainly circumstantial proof that Jesus was married to Magdalene and that there is no incontrovertible proof that says he wasn't. Researchers say they need cold hard facts, and I can respect that viewpoint, but some of these same researchers put forth the Bible as the absolute truth. Most serious researchers already know that the Bible has been edited and rewritten numerous times. How can you trust the Bible? The answer is simple—you can't. It has been tampered with and written by man.

The first five books of the "Old Testament" have been handed down for thousands of years in Judaic tradition and are known as the Torah. The first four books are believed to be God's direct and divine dictation to Moses (Genesis, Exodus, Leviticus, Numbers) while the fifth book (Deuteronomy) is believed to have been written by Moses just before his death, to give the Judaic people a set of laws to follow. (Author's note: Although there are varying theories on the Bible's makeup, I offer the theories that are most commonly accepted regarding the Bible.) These first five books are generally accepted to have been written at about 1200–1250 B.C.E, or more than ten centuries before any books of the New Testament. Some believe that these books were slightly edited or added to by Joshua or some other Judaic prophet in subsequent years. With the Judaic propensity for detail and subservience to God, most believe these additions were for clarification and that these writings are for the most part handed down as originally written. Most scholars believe, however, that the Old Testament was not put together in its entirety until about 400–200 B.C.E.—which is known as the era of scribes like Ezra. The Torah is the holiest of Judaic writings and is the cornerstone of the Judaic religion. Other writings have influence, like the Talmud (which is essentially a rabbinic book on Jewish laws, ethics, customs, and history), but the Torah is the heart and soul of Judaism. Both Christians and Muslims consider the Torah to be a divine work in their religions, as Christians include the Old Testament in their Bible and Muslims just consider the Koran (Qur'an) to be an update on these writings.

Most scholars say the Old Testament of the Bible is basically divided into three types of books—Law (Torah), Prophecy (books by prophets), and Writings (psalms, wisdom books, etc.). All of the writings of the Old Testament were completed before any writings in the New Testament. Most biblical scholars are divided into three camps: biblical maximalists, biblical minimalists, and those in between. Maximalists believe that the Old Testament is totally true and historical. Minimalists believe that the Old Testament is not historically accurate and many times allegorical in its writings. Those in the middle believe a bit of both. As of the date of this writing, many of the stories in the Old Testament cannot be proven, archaeologically or otherwise, and some archaeological evidence is actually in contradiction to some Old Testament writings.

Although Christians have accepted these Judaic writings into their Bible, over the years there has been much controversy. Many Christians, while acknowledging the divinity of the first five books and accepting the Ten Commandments as doctrine, have more or less divorced themselves from having to follow many of the Judaic laws. They say that Judaic laws don't apply to them because Christ made a new covenant with God based on mercy and forgiveness. I myself would probably be considered a biblical minimalist as I believe Genesis is almost completely allegorical in nature and I don't believe in the vengeful, wrathful, and petty emotions of God as portrayed in the Old Testament. The God portrayed in the Old Testament is not perfect, not all-loving, and certainly not all-merciful. Interestingly enough, early Gnostics also saw these disparities and even theorized that there were two Gods— one good and one bad—with the bad God creating man and the earth and all its negativity. The Gnostics of today don't share the beliefs of the early Gnostics of many years ago—we believe in a Mother and Father God who are all-loving, all-merciful, and who created us in Their image— male and female, just as we see in all of nature today.

I have always found it very hard to incorporate the Old Testament into my belief system because of the kind of God it portrays. To be honest, I don't accept much of what the Old Testament says except for some interesting historical stories. Even then, though, the parting of the Red Sea and stories like it are hard to accept ... so I don't. I do, however, admire the Judaic people as a whole because their fight against adversity and persecution has been a long one and entirely undeserved. The Judaic faith has devoted and staunch followers, and as a proponent of religious tolerance I believe everyone should be able to worship God(s) in their own way without the fear of persecution and bigotry. All religions have some truth and should be respected for that truth. To try and overtly convert people to a religion by conquest, persecution, terrorism, or fear is wrong.

Real conversion is made through one's own free will. You must study the various belief systems and pick the one that feels right for you. I am finding that more and more people are becoming religious, but not "religionistic." By that I mean they don't necessarily go to a church, temple, or mosque. They instead find themselves still believing in God but incorporating their own belief system because they don't believe in a lot of the dogma religions have instituted. That's why I founded my church, Novus Spiritus (New Spirit), because it essentially has no dogmatic rules to speak of, other than to love God and to follow the Golden Rule of "do unto others as you would do unto yourself." It is simple and yet effective because even though we put forth beliefs (such as a belief in both a Father and Mother God), those beliefs are informational beliefs that help a person to understand God and to get answers that are not only plausible but logical. For example, our belief in reincarnation gives plausible reasons for the inequities we see in life (such as poverty, short life span, lack of opportunity, etc.) as well as understanding the mercy of God—for He/She gives us more than one opportunity to advance our soul and learn from our mistakes. To that point, "sin" is nothing more than being ignorant of spirituality. The truly spiritual person knows the difference between right and wrong, and even though the most spiritual may fall and succumb to flesh, greed, jealousy, and other things once in a while, their spirituality comes back with a vengeance and puts them back on track. Even our Lord says the best of men falls ten times a day. Knowing this, I wanted to found a church where one could go and worship God with total peace of mind and soul. Our beliefs being informational in nature, we can then say truthfully, "Take with you what you want and leave the rest behind."

Not having the resources of major religions, we don't have that many branches of our churches, but we do have study groups (I always like to call them miniature churches) that can be formed or joined. There are hundreds of our study groups around the world, and if you are interested, you only have to contact us through the Internet or by phone.

I'm convinced that until he left home, Jesus was influenced highly by Mary. Even though Joseph was alive at this time in his life, we can see her influence in the way Jesus loved and supported women. I'm sure his rich memories of childhood and family life were part of his teachings. *"Unless you be converted, and become as little children, you shall not enter into the kingdom of heaven"* (Matt. 18:3). This is telling on two levels, reflecting his love of childhood and the simplicity of how we live, as well as how he wanted us to love God without complication. His parables and teachings showed his esteem for the faith and patience of women and condemned the injustices done to them by the male-dominated society of his time. His advocacy and appreciation of women surely came from and was nurtured by his love and respect for them. This came from his mother Mary, and he was also very sensitive to widows after Joseph died.

I also believe that Jesus's love for his own religious tradition and his ability to be critical of that tradition was due to Mary instilling honesty and a sense of devotion in him. The scriptures can be less than enlightening at times, but there is no doubt that Mary had a profound effect on his teachings (as almost all mothers do) and led him not only to the love of and marriage to Magdalene, but to his elevation of her as his disciple. He tried to bring out the true strong nature of women and went against the radical put-down of women that the Old Testament portrays.

His rejection by his own people gave Mary deep sorrow. She fought for him and sided with him when even some of his own relatives thought he had gone mad and wanted to seize him. She overcame many of these obstacles with her strength and eloquence. She never forgot that when she presented the baby Jesus at the Temple (Jewish law required a sacrifice to God be made by the mother and the circumcision of the male child), Simeon the Rabbi had predicted that a sword would pierce her soul over her son. She felt this when she foresaw the rejection and pain that he would experience in bringing the true God of love forward against the wrathful and vengeful God of Judaism.

Mary also instilled a love of humanity within Jesus. One day when he was preaching he was interrupted and told that his mother and brothers were seeking him. He said, "Who are my mother and my brothers?" Looking around, he then plainly said to the crowd of listeners, "Here are my mother and my brothers. Anyone who does the will of God, that person is my brother, and my sister, and my mother." Just in these short sentences we see how he loved his family and gave honor to women—especially his mother.

He honored Magdalene in the same way, which just enhanced the role of togetherness between Magdalene and Mary. Mary was the matriarch and would often treat the disciples as her children, while Magdalene was the partner, teacher, and disciple. Both roles complemented each other because both had as their focus or mission to help Jesus with his mission. No two people had any greater influence on him than these strong women.

We also know that Mary followed her son with Magdalene in his public life, because when he traveled through Galilee to Jerusalem the Bible tells us many shouted at Jesus, "Blessed is the womb that bore you and the breasts that nursed you." Mary was pleased but, even with her optimism, still was enough of a visionary to know that pain and heartache were ahead of him. I'm forever getting a little ahead of myself, but when Jesus and his disciples went up to Jerusalem to celebrate the Passover before his arrest, Mary followed him with Magdalene, relatives, and friends. She was very aware that danger awaited them there. Magdalene was also aware because, being more among the people, she was privy to the unrest and the rumors that circulated. The three of them knew they were in this trial together, and in some small way they knew that having each other and giving each other strength was some consolation. To face tragedy alone is terrifying, but the edge is taken off when you not only have hope of survival, but are also in concert together in empathy and giving each other comfort and solace. If Magdalene wasn't by Jesus's side, she would walk with Mary's arm leaning on her. Jesus loved the fact that the women he loved the most were close; it certainly made his life easier.

In Matthew 13:55–56, it is put forth that Jesus did indeed have brothers and sisters: *"Is not this the carpenter's son? Is not his mother called Mary, and his brethren James, and*

Joseph, and Simon [also called John], *and Jude* [also called Judas]: *and his sisters, are they not all with us? Whence therefore hath he all those things?"* In Matthew 27:55–56 it says, *"And there were there many women afar off, who had followed Jesus from Galilee, ministering unto him: among whom was Mary Magdalene, and Mary the mother of James and Joseph, and the mother of the sons of Zebedee."* The reason I even mention this is not only to show the closeness of Mary and Magdalene but also to show that besides his disciples Jesus had quite a clan of support from family members and friends that would have fit into the Judaic way of life to form close bonds. This carried through from the time of his childhood, when Mary was always the mother figure, both to her own immediate family and to cousins and friends. Her door, so to speak, was always open.

Magdalene's life was happier with her love for Jesus and Mary, and like many of us, she felt there were never any other options but to do what she was doing. This was her Chart, and if she followed it with constancy and endurance as well as giving love and support, she was fulfilling her destiny. No matter how hard it was, there was also satisfaction and joy. Most of us feel this in our wandering around until we find our niche. So in some ways, as hard as it was, she never had any other dreams of doing anything else.

If we could just put our lives on a spiritual road and stay on that road no matter what good or bad follows, we would have purpose and know that this life is temporary and transient. We would then keep our eyes on what is really our mission in this life—to follow the simple "love your neighbor as yourself" and "have love for God." Do this and you'll get through everything. God wants us to be happy even though we are in a hell here, but more importantly if you don't drop anchor in your own pain, self-pity, and hopelessness, you can then follow the simple road of what Jesus taught and exhibit the strength that both Mary and Magdalene showed in their lives. Mary lived for the day. Magdalene, being more complex, tried to plan every step, but even then there was a balance. Like I said before, Jesus was the head of the arrow, but they were the shaft and feathers that helped the mission move.

Mary didn't know exactly what was going to happen, but felt it in the atmosphere. With Magdalene, she had experienced Jesus's public life, the exultation and the defamation. On the first day of Passover, she and Magdalene watched his triumphant ride into Jerusalem on a donkey with all the fanfare as if he were a celebrated king who had come from a long journey. They squeezed each other's hand tightly, pleased that he finally seemed to be accepted, and yet there was tension in the air. Mary, above all, knew how fickle humankind can be.

Mary went ahead to get a room for the week of Passover. She secured a place in the Essene quarter, in an inn that had a large room overhead and could hold all the family and friends. The only thing Jesus had said was that things would not be what they seemed to be, and in the end they would all be together.

Mary did have faith, as she always did, but Magdalene felt that this could mean they would all meet in the kingdom of heaven. Mary felt that this, whatever it was, could not be the end, because she felt Jesus's message had not gone far enough, and after just three years the disciples were not prepared in courage or knowledge to be left on their own.

Several days later our Lord went off by himself to pray, and Magdalene and Mary had their own prayer circle.

Great preparations were under way for the final Passover dinner and celebration that was to take place in several days, and they also made preparations for a dinner that evening to celebrate their entry into Jerusalem. Neither Mary nor Magdalene realized at the time that the dinner this evening was to hold the significance that it would. Only Jesus knew, after he came back from his communion with God. Their guests all arrived around 5 P.M. Jesus, unlike Leonardo's portrayal of the last supper, reclined, as all of them did, on a bench that was padded with woolskins. Magdalene sat at the right, next to Jesus, and Mary was to his left with the family and disciples.

Jesus was aware of what lay ahead of him not only from his Chart, but also because he knew he had to fulfill scripture and his mission for God. Being human, he had already implemented steps to put Pilate's plan into action, but he didn't really feel that it would be successful and he believed that he would not live on. In his recent communion with God he'd anguished a bit over the fact that God was silent on the matter, but correctly perceived that this last test was a matter of faith on his part. At the dinner he tried to give them all courage and knowledge to carry with them, and the atmosphere became somewhat somber. No one there missed the subliminal language of his saying a type of good-bye, not only physical but emotional, with the hope that they would carry on and most of all be brave. This was especially so when he told them to eat bread and drink wine in remembrance of him. He meant it not as a sacrament per se, but as a coming together and staying together in their beliefs. His announcement that someone would betray him only confirmed to all of them there that they might not ever see him again. The room was filled with apprehension and fear, and Jesus did his best to calm them and bolster their spirits.

It seems Peter was not a brave man early in his life. He was filled with the fear that he would be imprisoned or worse because he was a follower of Jesus. We can therefore see the intuitiveness of Jesus when he told Peter he would deny him three times before the cock crowed. Peter protested that he would not deny Jesus, but according to the Bible that is indeed what happened.

Jesus was very affectionate toward Magdalene in public, but even more so this night. He felt like a condemned man, and the human part of him wanted to take solace in the love they both shared. The dinner was not jovial, but what one might feel as silently holy. Eventually, a kind of peace fell over the group. Of course, Passover is a time of reflection, but it had several days to go yet. Jesus was Gnostic in nature and was an Essene, but he still practiced the rules of Judaism and the laws of Moses. This just shows Jesus's liberation and his intention to seek after all truths and embrace all, as Magdalene and Mary did. The last supper took place in the Essene compound on Mount Sion, which was also known as the Temple Mount. After the supper, Jesus left with his disciples and walked around the city of Jerusalem almost as if he were saying good-bye to the city that meant so much to him. Mary and Magdalene were by Jesus's side with a hollow feeling of fear. Jesus, who was usually lighthearted, with a great sense of humor, was silent. Magdalene asked him if he wanted to talk; he declined. Then they made their way to Gethsemane. He prayed and talked to his disciples, giving them instructions about his teachings. After that, while walking in the garden, his brother came to him and kissed him (this was all part of the plot to save his life in which Jesus, Pilate, Judas, and Joseph of Arimathaea were involved) and soldiers of the Sanhedrin seized him. The reasons for the arrest were vague, but many felt he was getting powerful enough to overthrow the government or maybe cause an uprising. His popularity was his downfall, so to speak, but how else could he get his message out? Magdalene tried to fight the soldiers off, and Mary silently watched and prayed as most of the disciples ran. Later on, Peter denied knowing Jesus three times before the cock crowed—something he never got over for the rest of his life.

I don't think Jesus and his disciples expected it to go this far, but the powers that be and mobs have thoughts of their own. Many people went on to blame the Jews, the Romans, and Pilate; but people should know that that part of the world was a tinderbox even then. Not only was the populace afraid and suppressed by Roman rule, but Jewish sects and rebels were starting to rear their heads. As in this day and age, there were skeptics, detractors, and enemies, not unlike what set off the Salem witch hunts. It still continues today, and I certainly have been privy to this personally.

Jesus was brought before the chief priest of the temple, and all the other priests and ancients of the Sanhedrin were also present. Mary and Magdalene kept vigil outside the temple as they huddled together alone in the dark, both trying to console themselves and each other. Mary would stroke Magdalene's hair when she cried. Then Magdalene would compose herself and would obsess and wonder about where Jesus's supporters and his disciples were. Mary, who was wise, would say they would come around; they were just afraid. The hours never seemed to pass. It was like they were in a state of suspended agony. Anyone who has ever had to sit by a loved one suffering or not knowing the outcome of a drastic situation or illness can empathize with the fear and the helpless feeling of impotency that these two women felt.

Inside the temple, Jesus was beaten and made to watch as numerous witnesses were brought forward to testify against him. He was questioned constantly and all night long by the high priest and the high priest's followers. You must realize that these priests were in fear of having their positions and power taken away. I don't think anyone really realizes, even today, the powerful impact of Christ's message on the people. If the priests of the Sanhedrin felt threatened by him, then his message must have had a powerful influence on the people; otherwise they would not have even bothered with him. At that time there were numerous rebel leaders who led small pockets of resistance against the Romans, but the Romans always exacted revenge on any who fought against them. The Romans were not overly concerned with Jesus, because he was known to be a man of peace. Their spies had already checked him out and knew he didn't lead any army of resistance fighters. The Sanhedrin, however, was evidently very concerned about him. We then have to ask the inevitable question: Why?

If we read between the lines of the New Testament, we can almost see why. The priests at the temple brought false witnesses, trumped up charges, beat Jesus, and tried to get him to incriminate himself by constantly questioning him. Evidently the message that Jesus was giving out was welcomed wholeheartedly by the general populace and threatened the stability of the Sanhedrin. If we read the four gospels, we constantly see Jesus berating the hypocrisies of the priesthood, and we can then see that people evidently started questioning the actions of the priests in their local temples. Attendance at the various temples would probably have decreased and money would not have been coming in as normal. Jesus's message of a loving and forgiving God was having more impact than anyone would have thought, considering the devotion and devoutness of the Judaic people. The priests felt they had to get rid of this threat to their position and livelihood at any cost. In other words, they were afraid of him. They were not only concerned about his message, which many times contradicted their own, but they were also afraid that he was the Messiah. If people found that out, they would flock to him in droves and this would negate the priesthood. The religious hierarchy wanted control and they were not about to give it over easily.

Jesus was kept in the hands of the Sanhedrin all night long and to his credit didn't capitulate to their questioning and beatings. Upon seeing that he was not wilting under pressure, the priests decided to take him to the Roman governor Pilate and charge him with sedition. Magdalene tried to round up the disciples for moral support and, by asking many people, finally found them sequestered in an upper room somewhere. Neither she nor Mary could persuade them to come out, except for John and James, who were already with Mary. Joseph of Arimathaea also came to see how Mary was faring and, without divulging the plot, told her Jesus would live if everything went as planned. He also informed her that Jesus had been charged with sedition and had been brought before Pilate for trial and judgment.

When Magdalene returned, she had already heard of his conviction on the streets. She tried to console herself with what Jesus had told her, but still agonized over the horrendous ordeal. Even though her faith in him never wavered, she kept questioning why someone who only did good could be so punished. Mary explained it was pro-phetic and written in the scriptures, which shows that our Chart has to be completed but it also can be modified. If he went through his crucifixion, it would fulfill scrip-ture and his Chart, but there was the option to modify the Chart so that he would suffer greatly but live.

Pontius Pilate fulfilled his bargain as best he could. Now, I don't want to give the impression that Pilate was a nice man, as he was heavily bribed by Joseph of Arimathaea to do this. He did, however, follow through on what he said he would do and so at least showed some honor. God had infused Pilate's wife with a dream about Jesus, and Pilate was highly devoted to her and respected her opinions. She told Pilate to not harm Jesus because of her dream, and I'm sure he took that into consideration when he decided whether or not he would cooperate. As the Bible relates, Pilate could find no fault in Jesus. His spies told him Jesus was not really a threat like so many other Jewish zealots who wanted armed rebellion against Roman rule. He then tried to stall for time by sending Jesus to the court of Herod for judgment, but as we all know Herod sent him back to Pilate. He then tried to free him by offering to free a prisoner in honor of the Passover tradition, but the priests had backers who screamed louder for the freedom of Barabbas than for Jesus. His fate was sealed. Pilate probably knew this might happen, and although he had to prescribe the standard sentence for sedition of flogging and crucifixion, he made sure his soldiers delivered the minimum number of lashes in the flogging and also made sure his soldiers had orders to try to keep Jesus alive on the cross.

The streets were filled with mobs of the dissenters, but there were also many sympathizers in the crowds. It was therefore a chaotic and arduous journey for Jesus in carrying his cross to the hill known as Golgotha, the site of the crucifixion. Mary and Magdalene, along with James, John, and Joseph of Arimathaea, followed Jesus as he carried his cross up the hills of Jerusalem to Golgotha. It was hot and the air was stifling with oppressive humidity. Magdalene was faint with heat and stress, and with what we know today, it is possible her electrolyte balance was off. Always the mother, Mary brought water and pieces of bread that she forced Magdalene to take, saying that they had to keep their strength up for what was to come. Magdalene tried to put her mind on the end result and not the moment, but to see a loved one struggling and beaten while trying to carry a heavy cross up long hills was almost more than she could bear. When he fell, Magdalene cried out, "In the name of God someone help him!" Joseph finally braved the crowd and helped Jesus carry the cross.

Many years ago, my guide Francine was telling a large group of people about the travails of Jesus in the carrying of the cross, the nails driven into his wrists (if they had been put in his hands they would have been pulled out by his weight), and his suffering on the cross. We record every trance Francine does, and when we listened to the tape as witnessed by many, we could hear crowd noises and weeping and wailing. All those who had been in the room knew there was no sound like that during the trance...it was like Francine was bringing forward from Records on the Other Side the time in which it happened.

As they climbed the hill known as Golgotha, Mary was helped by Magdalene and James. They couldn't see the nails going into the wrists because of the crowds, but they could hear the pounding and the moans. Mary and Magdalene, in their empathy, felt the pain. Mary's hands started to bleed, which was probably the first stigmata. A stigmata is a real simulation of the wounds of Christ. It has shown up in numerous people over the centuries, like Father Pio, who was a devout Catholic priest known for his healing powers and stigmata manifestations. These simulations almost miraculously appear on someone who has a great devotion to Jesus.

Magdalene was weak with pain. Then they saw the cross raised and were stunned with agony when they saw the pain in Jesus's face. Joseph of Arimathaea approached them, and even though his face looked tormented by suffering, he informed them that all was going as planned. This was of some consolation to both Magdalene and Mary, but compared to how Jesus was suffering it seemed to be small at the time. Joseph had made a contractual agreement to take Jesus down from the cross after his supposed death and lay him to rest in his expensive tomb hewed out of rock with a rock door. It was he who had told Pilate it was meant for himself, but that he would donate it for Jesus's burial. This would ensure his so-called resurrection, rather then being buried in the ground alive to then die of suffocation.

As Magdalene and Mary stood at the foot of the cross, three hours seemed like weeks. John held Mary, and Magdalene was supported by James. Joseph of Arimathaea was standing by to immediately take Jesus down from the cross at sundown per Judaic law. When they finally took him down at sunset, both Mary and Magdalene rushed to him and with the help of the men got him to the tomb. Joseph checked for a pulse as he explained to the women that Jesus had been given an elixir to make him unconscious, to simulate death. Anxious moments passed and Joseph then exclaimed, "Praise be to God, he is alive!"

They tended to him quickly, as Mary had a great deal of knowledge in herbal remedies. They bathed him and cleaned and wrapped his wounds. Even though he was in bad condition, they were relieved. They had to do this quickly because there were guards from the Sanhedrin and witnesses outside the tomb who expected the tomb to be sealed. Thankfully, all the guards and witnesses thought that Mary and Magdalene were only cleaning and anointing the body per custom and didn't want to disturb the family of Jesus in their final good-bye, so to speak. Mary and Magdalene left him to rest while they went out from the tomb and settled under an olive tree to watch the tomb being sealed. Before the tomb was sealed, Joseph left food and drink for Jesus hidden in his linen wrappings. Magdalene insisted on keeping a vigil, and Mary left to tell the rest of the disciples that Jesus was all right. Jesus himself was in pain but had returned to consciousness. Although he was still somewhat groggy, he knew he had to feign death until the tomb was sealed.

You must realize that part of the prophecies in the scriptures regarding the true Messiah entailed his death and then his resurrection after three days. The Sanhedrin and their priests wanted to make sure that his disciples did not steal his body and then claim he had been resurrected, so they posted soldiers to guard the tomb for three days to ensure that didn't happen. Privately, they also wanted to make sure Jesus was not the true Messiah, and guards would report any strange occurrences that happened. Jesus was put in the tomb on Friday evening, and Saturday was the Sabbath and last day of Passover. All followers of the Judaic religion were expected to honor the Sabbath, but especially honor the last day of Passover.

Now, the Bible says that an angel appeared and frightened the guards of the tomb away, but that is not what really happened. Jesus knew he had to spend at least twenty-four hours inside the tomb because the plan called for him to be rescued at night or early morning when it was dark. In order for him to fulfill prophecy, the earliest he could be "resurrected" would be on Sunday, the day after the Sabbath. The plan called for him to wait as quietly as possible until Joseph of Arimathaea arrived to get him. This would be sometime in the darkness of the night of the Sabbath or the early morning of the next day. Everything was planned so that upon the morning of the day after the Sabbath, Jesus would be safely out of the tomb and in hiding.

Joseph related all of this to Mary and Magdalene. He stressed, however, that both of them must honor Judaic law and custom for the Sabbath and should not go near the tomb. Joseph was just being careful, and certainly didn't want anything interfering with their plans. He especially didn't want to risk Mary or Magdalene being seized or harassed because they were part of Jesus's immediate family.

Francine says that Joseph initially thought about bribing the two guards who were at the tomb, but then decided against it. If one or both refused the bribe, they might get suspicious and have the tomb opened to check the status of Jesus. He finally decided to give the guards an opiate that would knock them out for a while. He had also considered just knocking them out physically, but again that might create a problem because then the Sanhedrin would say that his disciples removed Christ's body. After the last guard change occurred at around midnight on the night of the Sabbath, Joseph arranged to have a pretty young girl wander by the tomb with a jug of wine that was heavily laced with a sleeping opiate. You can guess what happened. The guards drank the wine and very quickly went into a deep stupor. Joseph and several men quickly rolled away the stone blocking the entrance to the tomb and escorted Jesus away to a place of safety. When the guards came awake at dawn, they found the stone moved and the tomb empty. They were terrified at what would happen to them, so they concocted a story about an angel frightening them away. The priests, upon hearing this story, quickly went to the tomb and saw that the tomb was empty. They then ordered the two guards to say that the disciples of Jesus had stolen the body, which is the story that was given out to the public. Amazingly, the guards were not punished. This was probably because the priests thought they might tell everyone that the story being given out was a complete fabrication.

At first light on the day after the Sabbath, Magdalene went to the tomb (she didn't know if Joseph had been successful or not). She found the tomb open and the guards missing (they were telling the priests about what happened). Fear seized her as she thought maybe the guards had discovered Jesus was alive and taken him away. As

I related previously, Jesus had put on a disguise and met Mary at the tomb just after she had talked to an angel.

Magdalene went with Jesus to the room above the inn, and Mary was already there. Mary had been feeling their approach and was fixing soup, fish, and wine. Jesus surprised everyone with his appearance, and Mary was elated that he looked so well for the ordeal he had been through. The disciples were dumbstruck, but Mary wouldn't let them have any discussion then. She and Magdalene wanted Jesus to rest and recover. He spent a little over a week in rest and recovery, but even then he was making plans to go to the Essene town of Qumran, as it was a safer hiding place. Joseph had already set off on his journey to Tyre to arrange the next phase of their escape.

This was the time that is related in the Bible, when Jesus showed his wounds to his disciples and told them that he was still alive. Notice how this time is related in the gospels as time he spent with the disciples *after* the resurrection. The church, in its editing of the gospels, could explain it no other way, and several gospels relate how Jesus appeared to the disciples but they didn't recognize him. They try to explain this as Jesus appearing in another form, but it was the fact that he was disguised that explains their lack of recognition. He was in hiding, and if he had been in the glorified body he would have had no need for disguises. We also know that he spent at least eight days in the immediate area after his supposed death, because that is when the disciple Thomas first saw him and had the famous incident of poking his healing wounds before believing it was him. Again, Jesus reiterates that he is alive and of flesh and bone. As he says in John 20:27, *"Put in thy finger hither, and see my hands; and bring hither thy hand, and put it into my side; and be not faithless, but believing."*

It was also during this time that his disciples received the Holy Spirit and the instructions from Christ to go out into the world with his message as apostles. Mary and Magdalene were told by Jesus to pack only what they needed, and they accompanied him to Qumran to wait for word from Joseph. Jesus used Magdalene a lot as a messenger to carry word and teachings to the apostles during this time of waiting.

Jesus stayed at Qumran for several months, and he was worried about his teachings being absorbed and taught correctly by his disciples. He emphasized that his teachings be written down in order that they remain pure. In his scholarly opinion, even the Old Testament had many human faults within its writings, even though it had been in existence for hundreds of years. Although his mission had been to fulfill the prophecies of the Messiah, he didn't much feel like one at times. He was pleased that his teachings had reached many people, but even so he knew human nature and knew that his words would be manipulated and changed over time. He also knew that as a Jew his teachings were considered subversive by many. In order for them to take hold in any significant way, his disciples had to go out into the world with them.

CHAPTER 4

History's Most Beloved Gnostics

W HEN JESUS GOT word from Joseph of Arimathaea that all was in readiness, he donned yet another disguise. He then left Qumran, and Mary and Magdalene were waiting for him. All three of them were somewhat heavy at heart to leave their country, but Jesus knew it was too dangerous to remain and in his gratitude didn't want to uncover the plot ensuring his survival. Judas, by the way, never hung himself. The Bible didn't know how else to deal with an assumed traitor than to have him commit this act. Not only did he not do it, but in that day suicide was very rare and almost unheard of, because of the views of the Judaic religion.

All three of them went to the inn in the Essene compound in Jerusalem to say good-bye to Jesus's disciples and to give them some last words. Jesus found he could move around fairly freely in disguise. The heat of the moment was diminishing, and the Romans had their own problems of keeping order: They were always on the lookout for internal strife and signs of rebellion. Jesus and his crucifixion had become yesterday's news. With all of the defamation, humiliation, and suffering he had endured, there still was a strong grassroots movement to keep his words alive and not just in the secular Gnostic sects.

When he arrived at the inn, all of the twelve followers and several other disciples were waiting for him. They had recovered from his first appearances mostly because Mary and Magdalene had assured them of his survival and they and Judas had told them about the successful plot. Magdalene and Mary had also taught them heavily while Jesus was in Qumran and bolstered up their courage to go out and preach these teachings. Magdalene, in particular, taught them many of the teachings of Jesus that they were not privy to, and this is outlined in her Gospel. She knew this was the right time because she and Mary both knew they would not come back to Jerusalem or that part of the world again. Jesus had traveled, but they had not. They trusted that Jesus knew his way around the known world. Jesus had made Magdalene "the apostle he loved most," and in his eyes she was his number-one apostle. Jealousy caused some of the apostles to attack her words and teachings, but as I related earlier Mary intervened as the wise mother and demanded that they respect her.

It was also about this time that Magdalene began to feel different and she immediately went to Mary. Mary looked at her closely and hugged her with tears in her eyes and said, "Daughter, you have a child growing in you. She will be strong and carry on after we are gone." Magdalene was overjoyed, but knew they had a long journey ahead of them and hoped it wouldn't hold them up. The fact that she was in the early portion of her pregnancy certainly made it easier.

It was hard for Mary and Magdalene to leave, because this part of the world was all they knew. Mary had to leave some of her children behind, but knew, as she always had, that her life was preordained to be with her son "the Messiah": the one that God sent to change the world. As I related earlier, she also knew she would never be back. This was a bitter pill, but again she knew where her destiny would lead her and that it was for the greater good. Besides, she had Jesus, Joseph of Arimathaea, two of Christ's disciples—James and Philip (her son James remained behind to head the church in Jerusalem), and most of all her beloved Magdalene, who was more daughter to her than her own. Not only were they kindred souls, but they were also charted to make Jesus's life easier. They never faltered, doubted, or questioned, but went where he went.

We must remember that Jesus was first and foremost a Jew. There were many different sects or schisms of belief in the Judaic religion, and the Essenes were just one of many. Most of his teachings still had a foundation in Judaic laws and traditions. We still see this today in modern Christianity, with Christians accepting the Old Testament into their Bible and obeying the Ten Commandments. What many don't realize, though, is that the first Christians were Jewish Christians. Jewish Christians followed Judaic tradition and laws but also believed in the teachings of Christ. Depending on the sect, they either believed that Jesus was divine, or believed that he was a man and a great prophet. These early Christians were deeply entrenched in Judaism, and eventually James, Jesus's brother, became the head of the Jewish Christian movement in Jerusalem. A Gnostic movement also came out of Jewish Christianity because the teachings of Jesus sometimes came into conflict with the teachings of Judaism.

An example of this was the outlook of Judaism on God, which was one of emotion. God could be loving and merciful, but God could also be wrathful, vengeful, and merciless. Jesus put forth the concept of an all-loving and merciful God. The original covenant with God by the followers of Judaism was one of obedience, the following of His laws, and devoutness in worship. If the people did not obey, were not devout in their worship, or failed to follow the laws, then God would punish them with His wrath. Then Jesus comes into life and teaches that God is loving and merciful. He still teaches people to follow the bulk of the laws, but with a more tolerant and forgiving outlook. He enjoins the people to live their lives as best they can and rants against hypocrisy. We see in his teachings that motive and intent always take precedence over the letter of the law. He says that in living as good a life as possible, forgiveness and the Kingdom of Heaven (the Other Side) await. His teachings simply boil down to "Love thy neighbor as thyself and love God with all your heart and soul"—simple, complete, and to the point.

Being a Gnostic, Jesus looked at the Judaic teachings, laws, and traditions and found holes in them. He tried to fill those holes and bring an understanding, loving, forgiving, and merciful God to the foreground. That is all that modern-day Gnostics try to do. Great civilizations have come and gone and many religious interpretations have come and gone, but the core of Christianity through Christian Gnostics keeps coming back and rising up to tell the truth. The simple truth—without church, dogma, rules, and most importantly without the vengeful, wrathful, and fearful God—is that we have a loving, perfect, merciful, forgiving God who is not judgmental and loves us all unconditionally. We are here to learn in our temple (body), which is the true glory that emanates the part of God that we are. (We'll see more of this a bit later in the

Gospel of Mary [Magdalene] and in writings from the book *The Other Bible* edited by Willis Barnstone.)

I touched on some of the beliefs of the early Gnostics a bit earlier, but I must put forth that in most respects the beliefs of modern-day Gnostics do not go along with the earlier Gnostic theories or teachings. Gnosticism at the time of Christ and shortly thereafter was very much more ascetic and restrictive than modern-day Gnosticism. Most Gnostics of that period believed that there were two Gods, one dark and one light. The dark God created man and the earth, and was responsible for all the negativity and suffering of humankind. The real Creator was the light God, who remained static and was loving and merciful. The dark God was the god of wrath and vengeance. To early Gnostics, this explained why the Old Testament God of wrath and anger was different than the true God of love and mercy brought forth by Christ. Early Gnosticism, like almost all religions at that time, was very ascetic in nature and very strict as far as rules were concerned. Many Gnostic sects, like the Essenes, were secular and kept to themselves. Unlike the modern-day Gnostic movement, they would subject themselves to ritualistic prayer, ceremonies, and punishments. They were in truth just as strict in their laws as the Judaic faith was, and in some cases maybe even more so. They also were very patriarchal in nature (as were all monotheistic religions at that time), and women were not allowed to participate. Many banned women due to their monastic and secular nature.

After it was basically crushed in the power struggle of early Christianity, Gnosticism not only went into decline but also into hiding. It took several centuries for Gnosticism to come back even in a small way, and many changes ensued in its philosophies. The most well-known group of Gnostics to emerge were the Cathars. They were then almost annihilated completely in the Albigensian Crusade enacted by the Catholic Church to rid the world of their influence. Gnosticism again went into hiding and has just reemerged in the last several decades. The current philosophies bear no resemblance to the early Gnostics'. They still put forth the concept of an all-loving, all-merciful, and all-forgiving God, but also have brought forth the Mother Goddess, who was suppressed by the patriarchal religions for several thousand years.

The misinterpretation or editing of the gospels in the Bible has set back the truth about Jesus for almost two thousand years. The gospels say that Jesus ascended into heaven after his supposed death from crucifixion and resurrection. My guide Francine says this was either completely misinterpreted or infamously edited by the early Church. The Essenes had a cherished nickname for their center at Qumran and that nickname was "heaven." She says the original writings said that Jesus "went" to heaven and not "ascended" or "rose" into heaven. The original gospels just used the nickname for Qumran, as the disciples also became Essenes and it was considered by them to be a term of endearment. The Essenes were very secular in nature, so it is not hard to understand that they felt that their main compound of Qumran was a "heaven" because they could have privacy, relax, and worship as they pleased. Located in a very remote and deserted area, Qumran was built to keep people out. It was monastic in nature, and except for rare instances, women were not allowed. It had living quarters, meeting and eating halls, and several baths for rituals of hygiene. It was not particularly large and perhaps housed several hundred people at the most, but it was private and no one bothered the Essenes there.

Magdalene had absorbed more knowledge from Christ's lectures than the disciples. She had also learned from the quiet times at night when she and Jesus would talk for hours and even sometimes until the sun came up. Jesus really gave her more knowledge than any of his disciples, and in speaking to her he didn't have to resort to parables (which he was noted for). She understood his meanings without the usage of them. He also intensified his teachings to all of his disciples, for he felt they were ready for it.

Many religious writings reside in the hands of the Catholic Church, in their private repositories. More have come to light in archaeological discoveries in the past century or so. These writings are generally apocryphal and/or Gnostic in nature. They give us somewhat of a clearer picture, or in some cases a cloudier picture, of religious thinking just before, during, and after the time of Christ. Many are so esoteric in nature that they sound like the gibberish of insanity, while others seem to give us more insight into who and what Jesus was. The Catholic Church tried to keep these writings secret and locked away for so many years, but God always has a way of making sure that truth rises up. It always seems to come at a time when the world needs it most. The recent discoveries near Qumran by the Dead Sea as well as at Nag Hammadi and other locations in Egypt have brought forth new writings. The most recent discovery of the Gospel of Judas in Egypt has given us a completely different picture of Judas than the one that is put forth by Christianity. It is just another example of how so many writings on theology were cast aside to meet the agenda of the early Christians.

I, as most of you know, am a Gnostic Christian. I am also aware, however, of the early Gnostic writings and am highly critical of many of them. Most people don't realize that Gnosticism, like Judaism at the time of Christ, and Christianity now, had many schools of thought and philosophy. Some of these different sects and philosophies were in direct contradiction to one another, and others were so esoteric in nature that as far as I'm concerned they are absolutely useless. Humankind has always leaned toward overanalysis and often confuses simplicity with ignorance. Just because a philosophy is simple in nature doesn't mean that it doesn't hold truth. Organized religions have always written tomes and tomes of useless dogma because they somehow think that the more complex an idea is the more knowledgeable it is. All it does is create more confusion for their followers. This leads to some taking control over others, which creates more chaos in the world.

One of the things that I love about Buddhism is that it is fairly simple in its philosophy. I can't say that about Christianity, which is why I'm a Gnostic. If I tried to follow the philosophies of early Gnosticism, I would be utterly confused by all of the esoteric manure that they put out. Gnosticism as I practice it today is much simpler and down-to-earth. It has its basis in knowledge and truth, but instead of trying to confuse our followers with complicated dogma it tries to enlighten them by answering any and all questions. We give answers—logical and plausible ones based on the knowledge that we have accumulated over many years of study and research. But here is the kicker: we don't condemn you or give you guilt if you don't accept them. We allow you to disagree. Some of you may ask, "How can you do that and keep your followers intact?" The answer is simple. Unlike most religions or churches, we believe that the truth of our philosophies is what keeps people coming back. Part of our philosophy has always been religious tolerance. If we tried to keep our followers through fear and controlling dogma, we would be going against our own philosophy and become hypocrites. We have built our church on the seeking of knowledge and are not fenced in by unmovable dogma. Consequently, we can be more flexible. If a new truth comes to the world through discoveries that are always taking place, we can incorporate that truth immediately without the worry that it will conflict with existing dogma.

You may then ask, "How can there be any stability in your church without rules or dogma?" Stability doesn't come from dogmatic rules, although most religions would like you to believe that. Stability comes from God and truth. How many of you have belonged to churches or a religion in which there were parts of their dogma that you either didn't agree with or didn't believe in? Most of you, in all likelihood, and then you absorb guilt and don't feel comfortable with your religion or belief. What kind of stability is that? Happiness in one's religious beliefs doesn't come from a church or a synagogue or a mosque or a temple—it comes from feeling good about what you believe in. You change from a person who has faith and hope in his or her beliefs to one who knows that what he or she believes is true. You feel it in your soul and your whole being. That is how I feel about my beliefs and why I feel so good in writing them down and giving them out to the world.

When he'd met with the apostles for the last time before his departure, Jesus left to make last-minute preparations. He instructed Magdalene to tell the apostles as much as she could in the short time they had, so the apostles would have courage. Magdala was not Mary's last name by the way, but her title. In Hebrew it means "tower," which fits into her role as being the first disciple.

In the Gospel of Mary she begins to give the disciples courage. Some writings see Magdalene going on without Jesus, but there are also writings that tell of this holy family traveling to Ephesus, Ankara, and eventually to England and France. The Mormons believe that Jesus even visited North America. Regardless, the main thing is that they traveled with Joseph, James, and Philip and finally set up residence in the south of France. This explains why for years afterward a large group of Gnostics would reside there, and why it became such a Gnostic stronghold.

The Gospel of Mary relates some of the last discussions that Jesus had with his disciples before they left. I am including portions of it here as put forth in the Berlin Codex. The first six pages of the book are missing, and this copy of the gospel starts with a question to Jesus:

"Will matter then be utterly destroyed or not?" The Savior replied, "Every nature, every modeled form, every creature, exists in and with each other. They will dissolve again into their own proper root. For the nature of matter is dissolved into what belongs to its nature. Anyone with two ears able to hear should listen!"

Here, "dissolve again into their own proper root" means going back to the Other Side, from whence it came:

Then Peter said to him, "You have been explaining every topic to us; tell us one other thing. What is the sin of the world?" The Savior replied, "There is no such thing as

*sin; rather you yourselves are what produces sin when
you act in accordance with the nature of adultery, which
is called 'sin.' For this reason, the Good came among
you, pursuing the good which belongs to every nature. It
will set it within its root."*

To give in to our own ego and adulterate our path—this
means you're not living up to your spirituality, which Jesus
kept telling his disciples was so simple. I think the next
phrase is so telling and hopefully many who have com-
posed dogma will listen:

*Then he continued. He said, "This is why you get sick
and die, because you love what deceives you ... Peace
be with you! Acquire my peace within yourselves! Be
on your guard so that no one deceives you by saying,
'Look over here!' Or 'Look over there!' For the child
of true Humanity exists within you. Follow it! Those
who search for it will find it. Go then, preach the good
news about the Realm* [the Other Side—the kingdom
within and without]. *Do not lay down any rule beyond
what I determined for you, nor promulgate law like the*

lawgiver, or else you might be dominated by it." After he had said these things, he departed from them.

This is where he left Magdalene for a short time to bolster the disciples up, as they were wavering because of his departure. He also left her to finish up his teachings, which he had given her, as we will see below.

But they were distressed and wept greatly. "How are we going to go out to the rest of the world to announce the good news about the Realm of the child of true Humanity?" they said. "If they did not spare him, how will they spare us?" Then Mary stood up. She greeted them all, addressing her brothers and sisters. "Do not weep and be distressed nor let your hearts be irresolute. For his grace will be with you all and will shelter you. Rather we should praise his greatness, for he has prepared us and made us true Human beings." When Mary had said these things, she turned their heart toward the Good, and they began to debate about the words of the Savior.

Peter said to Mary, "Sister, we know that the Savior loved you more than all other women. Tell us the words of the Savior that you remember, the things which you know that we don't because we haven't heard them."

Mary responded, "I will teach you about what is hidden from you." And she began to speak these words to them.

The only way this could happen is that Jesus spent long hours alone with her telling her his thoughts and beliefs. It also shows that after his supposed death, he was going to keep a low profile. He would feed her information so he could be in the background and she would come to the foreground as his mouthpiece.

The gospel then goes on, with Mary relating to the disciples that she saw the Lord in a vision. There is another whole section that is missing, and the gospel begins again with Magdalene giving out more teachings from Jesus—this time the tail end of a discourse on the soul talking to different powers represented by Desire, Ignorance, and Wrath in its ascent to heaven from death. It almost has a parable-like dialogue and the end of it, which speaks of eternal rest:

The soul replied, saying, "What binds me has been slain, and what surrounds me has been destroyed, and my desire has been brought to an end, and ignorance has died. In a world, I was set loose from a world and in a type, from a type which is above, and from the chain of forgetfulness which exists in time. From this hour on, for the time of the due season of the aeon, I will receive rest in silence."

We see here how the soul of the individual, in its ascent to heaven, is no longer bound to the earth plane. All earthly desires fade away and the knowledge of the soul comes back fully after the shackles that block memory for those on earth drop away.

After Mary had said these things, she was silent, since it was up to this point that the Savior had spoken to her.

Here we see that Magdalene only teaches what she has been told by Jesus to teach and does not try to elaborate on the teachings. This was one reason why he trusted and loved her so much, for she never let her ego override the instructions that were given to her by him. Jesus knew he didn't need to speak in public anymore because he had Magdalene to carry on. It was also more dramatic to finish his public life on a sacrificial note and let her continue.

Andrew responded, addressing the brothers and sisters, "Say what you will about the things she has said, but I do not believe that the Savior said these things, for indeed these teachings are strange ideas."

Peter responded, bringing up similar concerns. He questioned them about the Savior; "Did he, then, speak with a woman in private without our knowing about it? Are we to turn around and listen to her? Did he choose her over us?"

Then Mary wept and said to Peter, "My brother Peter, what are you imagining? Do you think that I have thought up these things by myself in my heart or that I am telling lies about the Savior?

Levi answered, speaking to Peter, "Peter, you have always been a wrathful person. Now I see you contending against the woman like the Adversaries. For if the Savior made her worthy, who are you then for your part to reject her? Assuredly the Savior's knowledge of her is completely reliable. That is why he loved her more than us. Rather we should be ashamed. We should clothe ourselves with the perfect Human, acquire it for ourselves as he commanded us, and announce the good news, not laying down any other rule or law that differs from what the Savior said."

After he had said these things, they started going out to teach and to preach.

No matter how simple you make an idea, people always want to detract out of ego, jealousy or, even more frightening, the attitude that "I know more than you because I am the privileged one." Jesus made all people equal and his teachings were simple, but humankind can't seem to let it alone and make it more complicated. They instill fear, retribution, and even occultism. Everyone should be able to research or even believe Jesus's words and just live accordingly.

We know historically that most of the apostles scattered and tried to spread the teachings of Jesus. Most of them were martyred in some way under Roman rule. We also know that Peter said he wasn't worthy enough to be martyred like Jesus, so he was crucified upside down. What most of the other apostles did, however, is vague. That's why the gospels of Thomas and James and Magdalene were so important, because they helped to fill the gaps of Jesus's teachings and propagate the far-reaching effects to keep his true teachings alive. These gospels were initially suppressed by the male-dominated early Christian church. Jesus's brother James stayed behind in Jerusalem and became the head of the main faction of the Jewish Christian movement. Research shows that James butted heads with both Peter and Paul many times over interpretation and religious dogma, which led to the schism between the Jewish Christians and the Pauline Christians that Peter embraced.

Magdalene left the group of disciples and went to find Jesus and the rest of the soon-to-be travelers—Joseph, James, Philip, and Mary. Francine says that after they had finally settled in France, they were joined by two others. Though this will be discussed later, Thomas and Levi eventually made their way to France to help Magdalene with her ministry. It's important to keep as true to the timeline as possible and to include the actions and the people that fit into the sequence of events.

Mary was busy getting ready while Magdalene and Jesus were giving pep talks to the apostles. Then they all set off in a caravan headed toward Tyre. Jesus had made a lot of acquaintances in the earlier travels of his youth, and he was looking forward to contacting old friends and teachers. Magdalene's early pregnancy didn't seem to hold up the travels, but by this time Mary's strength was starting to give out and she was often carried on a litter or rode a pack animal. She still had the caring and love and optimism in her demeanor as well as her mental acuity. Magdalene tended to her every wish to always make her comfortable. Jesus and Magdalene noticed that the advent of the birth of a grandchild gave Mary's life new meaning. It gave her a joy that she hadn't had for a long time because of all the worries over her son. They all were in a spirit of adventure. Francine says that at this point they weren't sure where they would end up or what place they would call home, so they kept all options open. The journey from Jerusalem to Tyre was not overly long, and about a week later they all were on a ship bound for what is now known as Turkey.

CHAPTER 5

The Great Pilgrimage

MARY DID SEEM to become more of a visionary as she got older. She would tell everyone where to go and how they would be received. She was always on the watch to keep them all away from detractors or anyone who would really know their whereabouts. The Roman Empire was in such a tumultuous state that I feel Jesus was just a piece of sand on a beach that was torn asunder with the tides of rebellion. It wasn't that Mary was paranoid, but once you have been traumatized it's hard to get over what we now know as post-traumatic shock or stress disorder.

Trauma can't help but follow you for some time. Mary, the ultimate protector, was always on the alert for any problems or any information that would get back to Jerusalem. Throughout *The Other Bible*, a book of ancient alternative scriptures, many visionaries proclaimed the wisdom and holiness of Mary, especially Isaiah. "She herself knew of her life" and this tells us that she saw before and after.

She was almost a barometer for human feelings and wisdom of spirituality in this life and the afterlife. I'm sure she was infused with knowledge because of her son, but she must also have been infused with her own knowledge, and she imparted this to Magdalene.

Valentinus was one of the most famous and renowned of Gnostic teachers and theologians in early Christianity— living from approximately 100 C.E. to 161 C.E. In *The Other Bible*, the section devoted to Valentinus and the Valentinian system says, "What suffered [speaking of crucifixion] was the psychic Christ, the one constructed from the constitution of the universe, in a mysterious fashion, so that through him the Mother might set forth the model of the Christ above." It also states that from the stem (which is

Mary) the seeds are her children (mainly Jesus). Similarly, the sayings of Jesus came partly through his divination and being a tube of infusion from God, which gave him revelation. Aside from the divine intervention that I believe is in all of us, you have to figure in his human DNA—especially in light of his life being a mission for God. Why would Mary have been picked as his mother if she could not foster this child or have gifts of her own? Wouldn't she then need to impart these gifts to the disciples and especially to Magdalene? It is evident that she did have these psychic gifts in her DNA, which were transferred to Jesus, and then were even more magnified by God. So the three of them made up a trinity of strength, infused knowledge, and psychic abilities that allowed them to know what road they should take. At the time it was to send the apostles out into the world to preach, put themselves into exile to plant seeds, and finally end up in France.

In their voyage to Turkey, they kept close to the shore and stopped in several ports where Jesus talked to friends he had made in his earlier travels. Some had heard that he was dead and were very happy to see that he was alive. To cover their tracks, so to speak, he briefly told these friends about his escape and asked them to keep his survival a secret. He certainly didn't want the Romans searching for him. Their ship arrived in the port of Ephesus in Turkey about a month after they had set sail. Ephesus was a major port at the time that led to trade routes to the Far East, and Jesus had many friends there.

As an aside, it was strange in my own travels to that area that all the people told me that the Anatola (the Mother God) was their ruling deity. She even shows up in their tapestries and rugs through the symbol of a woman with hands on her hips. In Turkey, in the area known as Anatolia (named after the Mother Goddess), they take for granted that Jesus, Mary, and Magdalene stopped there. When I was in Ankara, one of the main cities there, I led a tour of about 270 people. There was a beautiful but somewhat decaying temple with spotlights on the rock formations, a string quartet that played soft music, and it was my birthday. Abass Nadim (the tour operator and a dear friend who has since passed away) held a birthday party for me there. I have to say that my birthday aside, this was the most holy night I have spent anywhere, and all of the people on the tour were in as much awe as I was.

We talked about the experience off and on through the rest of the tour, and that uplifting of the soul made the rest of the trip anticlimatic.

The Other Bible is a compilation of ancient religious scriptures that are either Apocrypha, Gnostic, or Jewish and contain wisdom texts as well as writings from the Dead Sea Scrolls. It's interesting to note they keep referring to the word "psychic" or "visionary" whenever Mary's name is mentioned. Whether it was prophecy in the Bible, the Witch of Endor that brings Samuel back from the dead to prophesize Saul's demise (which did happen in battle), the many prophets such as Daniel, Isaiah, Ezekiel, etc., or the oracles in Greece, psychic ability was accepted in ancient times. It was considered a matter of fact that some men and women could foretell the future.

Psychic ability is still respected and revered in other countries. I know this firsthand, as most of their religious beliefs are centered on prophets (like Mohammed and the prophets of the Old Testament). These older religions still pay homage to prophets, and it was in this country alone that we had a division in belief. This is possibly because our beliefs are so varied and complicated and we are not so simplistic, being more into technology and getting ahead. Both have their pros and cons. If we let every nut here gain prominence, then we see a rise in occultism, which I abhor. We also see side-street psychics with flashing hands or people on the Internet advertising that they can remove curses for thousands of dollars. There doesn't seem to be any way to stop it. Many of these charlatans have even used my name to advance their phony schemes. I have had lawyers and district attorneys working on these people using my name, but it's a daunting task and skeptics like to use me as fodder with their inflammatory views and false statements. A part of my soul feels empathy for Jesus, Magdalene—who has been branded a whore untruthfully—and Mary, who was swept under the proverbial rug with a little acclaim here and there and then fell through the cracks of patriarchal rule.

While in Ephesus, Jesus rented a house where they all could live. After several months, he sent Joseph of Arimathaea to England to preach and establish a community much like the Essene communities in Israel, but without the rigidity of laws and traditions that the Essenes followed. He told Joseph to come back to Ephesus in three years' time. Joseph then set sail for England and checked on his mines. As we know, he also started a religious community at Glastonbury.

Mary was getting older and somewhat more frail. The trauma of Christ's arrest, trial, and crucifixion and the frantic days of hiding in fear of Jesus being recaptured had taken their toll. She needed a long rest, but Jesus was anxious to travel and renew friendships he'd cultivated in other lands years earlier. It was decided that Mary would remain in Ephesus with James as her protector, and Jesus, Magdalene, and Philip would travel to India. Jesus had thought about leaving Magdalene behind with his mother, but Magdalene, with her fiery disposition, told him in no uncertain terms that she was going with him. He tried to use her pregnancy as an excuse to leave her behind, but she would have none of it, telling him that the baby she had inside of her would survive a little travel. Mary, as much as she loved Magdalene and didn't want to be parted from her, actually took her side in the brief argument. She knew how much Magdalene loved Jesus and also knew how unhappy she would be if she was parted from him, baby or no baby. So with Mary safely in a comfortable house with James to look after her, Jesus, Magdalene, and Philip started their journey to India.

The journey was slow for several reasons. Jesus was very aware of Magdalene's pregnancy and didn't want to overtax her, and he also stopped along the way to meet with friends and teach. He felt much more comfortable teaching in this area because most of the religions practiced by the inhabitants were pagan in nature. They first traveled through the Anatolia region of Turkey and then caught on with some caravans that were going into what is now Iraq and stayed for several weeks in Mari. They then pushed on to Nippur. It was in Nippur that Magdalene gave birth to their first child, a girl, and they named her Sarah. They stayed for over a month in Nippur to let Magdalene and Sarah gain strength. They then traveled eastward through what is now known as Iran and then through Afghanistan into Kashmir. They made their base in the city of Srinagar in Kashmir, and Jesus rented a house so that Magdalene and Sarah would be comfortable. It was from here that Jesus then traveled into the surrounding areas of Kashmir and India to teach. They stayed there for almost one-and-a-half years. As the journey there had taken almost a year, it was then time to return to Ephesus not only to reunite with Mary, but to meet Joseph at the appointed time. Five months later they were back at Ephesus, and the reunion with Mary was a very happy one. The rest had done her good, and despite an almost three-year separation, she seemed to be in good health.

Mary was ecstatic over her grandchild Sarah, who was now about two-and-a-half years old, and the child quickly became the joy of her life. This is what she had been living for. Through all of her trials and a hard, sorrowful life, she kept steady and optimistic. Her optimism came into full bloom not only in seeing the bloodline continue, but in having joy in this time of her life in the form of a beautiful, dark-eyed, curly dark-haired granddaughter. She literally took over her care and feeding from Magdalene, and both Jesus and Magdalene laughed about how she was such a doting grandmother. Sarah was close to all of them, but especially to Mary, who from early on began to teach her all the precepts of her father's and later her mother's teachings. Mary was so glad that her son and daughter-in-law had returned and were safe. They were finally back together after almost three years, and Mary vowed to herself that they would not be separated again.

Magdalene was also joyously happy to see Mary again and had missed her terribly. The joy of their reunion was emphasized by their almost shameful neglect of Jesus. Jesus laughed about the fact that they were constantly yapping away at each other in catching up on what had transpired while they were separated. Jesus was also happy at seeing them reunited and so involved with each other. He took this time as an opportunity to go out to meet with friends and to make preparations for their departure after Joseph arrived.

Joseph of Arimathaea arrived with their ship about two weeks later. He was in good spirits not only at seeing them all again, but as he reported to Jesus his mines in Britain were flourishing and the settlement at Glastonbury was a huge success. As I touched on earlier, to me Joseph was the biggest hero in this whole scenario. He not only instigated the plan for Jesus's survival, but carried it out to perfection. He then arranged their escape, and it was carried off flawlessly. Last of all, with his wealth he financed the bulk of the expenses of the group. In addition, he started the religious community at Glastonbury and taught the teachings of our Lord to many with pagan beliefs. He was a true and ardent follower of Jesus, and unlike the twelve disciples in the Bible (Joseph was also a disciple, actually), he showed courage in the face of danger and had an uncanny ability to get things done—and done right. This was probably due to the fact that Joseph had dealt with Rome, knew Roman administrators' nuances, and was a very capable trader and businessman.

About a week later, they all boarded their ship and again sailed off, this time to Greece. They were all following the directions that Jesus gave. He had wanted to meet and make contact with some of the holy men and teachers whom he had listened to in his youth and early travels. With these subsequent travels he found that many of his old friends and teachers had died, but that didn't deter him. It was almost as if he was trying to squeeze out the last bit of knowledge that he could get before he finally settled down someplace. From Greece they went to Italy and Egypt. While in Egypt Jesus brushed up on the teachings of the ancient mysteries. They then set sail for

Britain, as Jesus wanted to see what Joseph had done in Glastonbury.

When they arrived at Glastonbury, Jesus was amazed at what Joseph had done in starting this new religious settlement. They stayed there for several weeks, and Jesus also roamed the nearby countryside, impressed with all the beauty of nature. Israel was dry and arid, and Britain was green and lush. They left Britain and sailed down the French and Spanish coast and went back into the Mediterranean. They went north and finally came to the south of France and landed in Messalia (now known as Marseille). They then spent several weeks getting the lay of the land. Jesus finally decided to settle west of Messalia in what is now known as the Languedoc region of southern France, near the small town of Rennes-le-Château. They bought some property in the area and Jesus took the name David Albengentun. Francine says Jesus was led to this area and felt it was the best place for them to settle. At that time this area was not under French rule but was a province called Gallia Narbonensis under Roman rule.

The people in this area were basically followers of various pagan religions, and Jesus kept a very low profile for two or three years. Magdalene then started her public life, which he monitored. Magdalene would take the women aside to teach them Jesus's teachings. As these teachings became more popular, she then taught them ceremonies and services that they could hold in their homes. Mary was almost always in attendance when Magdalene taught and many times would contribute to the teachings. She was like the conscience on the validity of what they were saying, and because she was older she initially had more respect, but Magdalene's fame as a teacher grew and grew. They were very successful in the area, and most of the inhabitants became the first true Gnostic Christians. The roots of these teachings went deep into the people of the area. Centuries later, this whole region was known to be a stronghold of Gnostic thought and philosophy.

Jesus, in the meantime, concentrated on teaching the children of the area. He had always found children to be open vessels in which knowledge could be firmly implanted. He knew that for his message to grow he needed the children to carry it on. He loved children, and very soon after they had settled Magdalene was expecting a second child. Magdalene and Jesus loved their little Sarah so much, but still had the passion and vision to keep their Gnostic beliefs alive: putting forth a loving, forgiving God and erasing all the fear instilled by the previous prophets or various religions. A second daughter, whom they named Esther, was soon born, and Mary became the doting grandmother to another child. Later on, Magdalene had two boys, and as she grew older also had three miscarriages. The children were a joy to them all, and as we will see Sarah remained with her mother until her mother's death.

Magdalene's teachings became more and more popular, and parents also raved happily about Jesus's teaching of their children. They were still trying to keep as low a profile as possible, but their fame soon spread and it was inevitable that word came to the region about the man in Israel named Jesus Christ and how he had died on the cross for teaching about a loving and merciful God. With the news about what kind of teaching this Jesus put forth, it was also inevitable that the people compared these teachings to the teachings that Magdalene and "David" put forth. Finding them so similar, the people started asking questions.

In the short time they had been in the area the people had come to love them greatly. They were popular not only for their teachings but also because they were kind, considerate, and always happy to lend a helping hand when needed. Mary and Jesus had healed many in the area from various illnesses, and so it was no wonder that they were not only respected but loved by their neighbors. Jesus, knowing this, finally decided to let the cat out of the bag. He gathered his neighbors together by holding a party, and when all had gathered he told them who he really was. At first the reaction from the people was one of doubt and fear. After he assured them that he was indeed the Jesus who had been crucified in Israel, all of them were amazed at his survival. He told them all what had happened—from their escape to their travels and to them finally ending up there in France to settle down. After relating all of their recent history, he only asked his neighbors to keep the secret of his true identity to themselves. None of them were happy under Roman rule, and all knew that the Romans thought he was dead, so the people vowed en masse to never reveal the secret about him and his family. This was not hard for them to do because Jesus was so loved and liked and he and members of his family had helped the surrounding community in so many ways.

Magdalene and Jesus went on with their teaching, and more and more people in the area became aware of the kind couple who spoke about a loving and merciful God. Most knew them as renowned teachers, and only their closest neighbors knew the real truth. Their life was very peaceful and rewarding. Jesus taught the children and started writing, and some of his writings were attributed to Philip and Thomas. Francine says much of his writing is still undiscovered or hidden away, but some will be discovered in the next decade or two. He also helped Magdalene write her gospel and helped several of his disciples with their writing. Some scholars thought that Jesus might have been illiterate, but as the Bible points out this is not true because he wrote in the sand (John 8:6, 8:8) when the unnamed adulteress was brought before him.

Jesus knew from his contact with God that it would be centuries before his words would be interpreted with spiritual simplicity and without the interference of power that would bury them instead. Both he and Magdalene were bringing the real truth to light, but history dictated that much of what they taught was changed and manipulated by man when Christianity fully came into being. Jesus and his mother probably both knew that his words would be buried and denied until the world was ready to hear them. All he could do then was teach, and the rest would reside with how history played it out. As fruitless as it sometimes seemed to be, Magdalene and Jesus persevered, taught, and kept a low profile.

Sarah became Mary's protégée because Mary lived long enough to impart great knowledge to her granddaughter. Although Magdalene also had Esther and two boys, they don't seem to show up in any religious writings whatsoever. Just as there is still controversy over whether or not Jesus had brothers and sisters, there is an ongoing controversy over whether Jesus was married and had children.

This is when the secrets began that were guarded by the Gnostics as well as by the Knights Templar later on. Though everyone was looking for the Holy Grail, it was the Holy Family that carried it. Mary carried Jesus in her womb, and Magdalene carried the bloodline of Jesus. One could say there were two grails—not the one Jesus drank out of. Honestly, who would care what kind of crude cup he drank out of? It seems to be a well-concocted story to start the Crusades which—sadly, over a thousand years later—degenerated into war, genocide, and plundering.

The family lived in a compound with a main house and several outbuildings. There were also many caves in the area, and it was in these caves that both Jesus and Magdalene taught. Later on, the Gnostic Christians also held religious services in them and used them as their first "churches." Even today there are cave paintings and even shrines in many of these caves, and some of the earliest Christian art shows Magdalene in a cave.

Some of Jesus's original disciples touched base or came and went. John, Levi, and Andrew visited, but then went on their way. No writings exist confirming these visits except that in his gospel, as well as in Thomas's and Philip's, the writer seems to know what Jesus wanted to say. We could say it was infused, but when one reads them these gospels give new and ongoing information. This is information that was never revealed in his public life while Jesus was alive and offers ongoing narratives of his words and what he wanted to impart to the world.

The house where Jesus, Magdalene, Mary, and the children lived did have several rooms and all the necessities of that time. They had a fireplace for cooking, and most of their food came from the surrounding community as gifts or recompense for Jesus and Magdalene's teaching and healing. They did have their own garden, where they would grow vegetables and they also had several goats, sheep, and chickens.

Mary the Visionary, as she is called in many texts, was coming to the end of her life. Why call her a visionary? Well, the very fact that she talked to the angel and was told she would have the Holy Spirit from God descend upon her and that she would give birth to the coming Savior is reason enough. But as I have related, she was constantly aware of the right direction to take, who to avoid in their travels, and always seemed to know things that were in the future.

Mary died very quietly about ten to fifteen years after they had arrived in the Languedoc region. She was in her early sixties while our Lord was in his late forties and Magdalene was in her late thirties. They had spent their whole lives together, and Mary was the only mother that Magdalene really related to. So as she lay quietly dying with Sarah, the other three grandchildren, James, Levi, Joseph of Arimathaea (who was about the same age as Mary), Jesus, and Magdalene in attendance, she was at peace. She felt she had completed her journey of life and that she had fulfilled her Chart. She didn't care if she would not be of real note (although as we know she is venerated highly all over the world). She only relied on her relationship with God, believing as I do that it doesn't matter what the world says or thinks; it is only what God knows and thinks that is important.

When her soul left her body, they all could see it ascend in pure, glorified form. There was mourning, of course. This included the family and all the surrounding groups of people who were not only Gnostics, but also people who didn't necessarily believe but admired Mary and her healing abilities. There was definitely a hole in everyone's life, though the largest impact was on Magdalene. She had lost her mother figure, her mentor, and her confidante. Jesus, who was closer to God, took it hard because in the flesh we still feel the selfish loss of having the departed with us. His grief, however, was minimized by his knowing that we will all end up together on the Other Side.

After Mary died, Magdalene threw herself into her

work and caring for her children. She had many friends, and several helped her not only in raising her children and doing cooking, but also in transcribing her teachings. History bears out that the Gnostics were learned and could read and write.

That's why it's so hard for scholars to figure out who really wrote what. If certain writing is attributed to a particular person, did that person actually write it? As I've stated, a prime example of this confusion is the four canonical gospels of Matthew, Luke, Mark, and John. Most laypeople believe that they were written by those four disciples, but valid scholars all disagree and no one really knows who wrote them. It is the same with the numerous apocryphal and Gnostic writings on the periphery of Christianity: no one really knows who wrote them. Even in the writings of Paul there are parts that have been labeled forgeries by scholars because they know he didn't write them. We can also pretty much surmise that this could be a problem in both the Old and New Testaments, because both were handed down by oral tradition. Oral tradition, in many cases, is like giving a thief a license to steal. It can be very undependable in that each person whom a story is told to can elaborate, put his or her own spin on it, and the message can get lost in translation. Unfortunately, in ancient times, there was a lot of illiteracy so oral tradition is often all that we have to go on.

Couple the renditions of oral tradition with the agenda of the early Christian Church and you have the makings of real history being turned into fictional history. It may sound heretical, but with all the new evidence coming out it is proving to be very true. Scholars already know that much of the New Testament was heavily edited by the early Church, and who really knows whether their sources were real, imagined, or correct? That is one reason why so many apocryphal and Gnostic writings are in conflict with writings contained in the Bible, because these noncanonical writings that were rejected by the early Church were not heavily edited. Why edit something that you are not going to include in your holy book?

The problem really gets down to this: only God knows. Even when I'm researching, it's awfully hard to not put my own spin on things. If I do, I write my own thoughts later and stick as closely as I can to the research text. The other problem with relying on ancient writings is that they were all written years and years after the original incidents occurred!

Imagine if you can that you are a writer and you are asked to write a history of World War II based only on the oral record of twelve World War II veterans. You can't use your own knowledge of events (they didn't have newspapers or history books in Jesus's day) and you can't use the historical knowledge that the veterans have picked up. You can only rely on what they tell you they experienced. Unless these veterans were in every battle and on all continents, you would find yourself getting a very narrow view of World War II. No matter how good a writer you were, your view would be limited and incorrect because it would be missing so much information. What makes you think that the rendition of the life of Christ as portrayed in the Bible would be any different? In my book *The Mystical Life of Jesus* I constantly point out inconsistencies in the four gospels as written and how there are many times that they conflict with one another. If the writers of the four gospels cannot even agree with one another, how can they be relied on? Now you see why I wrote *The Mystical Life of Jesus* and why I'm writing this book.

CHAPTER 6

The Church That Won

I HAVE DONE SOME traveling of the world, and in
doing so I was constantly amazed at how Mary, Magdalene, and Jesus were venerated in areas that are predom-
inately not Christian. I found this to be especially true in
Egypt and Turkey. It just shows that if you speak spiritually
rather than dogmatically, everyone comes to a common
ground. The love of all ideas, theories, and sensible solu-
tions to problems that have bedeviled humankind since
before written history will always find an audience. They
are constantly finding old writings such as those at Nag
Hammadi and Qumran that are giving us new insights

and new gospels, such as the Gospel of Mary, the Gospel of Thomas, and the Gospel of Judas. Before the end of this decade we are going to see more discoveries coming to the public eye that tell us more about not just the woman's place, but the spiritually kind teachings of Jesus. Archaeologists are now trying to acquire more information and piece it together. The History Channel recently had a program that was citing these newly discovered writings, and some were even found in an Egyptian bazaar.

People in Turkey strongly insist that the holy family visited there and lived there for a time. Many in India and Kashmir speak of the great teacher and prophet Jesu and again put forth that Jesus was there. Magdalene is venerated highly in southern France, and English legends are full of Joseph of Arimathaea bringing Jesus to Britain. In that time and in these various areas Jesus didn't make many converts, but that was probably because he was just planting seeds of his philosophy. Even though most weren't converted, there was a great liberal understanding of his words. His veneration and respect in these areas raise questions because other than the Bible saying that Jesus was taken to Egypt as a baby, Christianity basically says

Jesus spent all his life in Israel. More and more research indicates that this is just not true. You then have to ask: why was and is this apparent falsehood still perpetuated?

If the Christian powers that be can put forth false information about how Magdalene was a sinner and prostitute (which they just recently recanted on) for almost two thousand years, what other secrets or falsehoods are they still hiding? Is the truth about Jesus, Mary, and Magdalene one of the greatest perpetuated hoaxes of all time? Were Jesus and Magdalene married and did they have children? Did Jesus live beyond his crucifixion? I personally believe that the answer to all of these questions is yes, and I think strong evidence will be forthcoming that proves that I am right. Right now there is a lot of circumstantial evidence that leans in this direction, but no conclusive or definitive proof. On the other hand, there is no conclusive evidence to the contrary, either, other than the New Testament in the Bible.

Over the years, scientific scrutiny of the Bible has had its ups and downs. On one side you have those who believe it is literally God's word, is infallible, and is an accurate and completely factual book with true accounts of history. On the opposite pole you have those who think it is pure myth and fantasy, and while it may contain some historical facts, they also point out its many shortcomings and falsehoods. Then you have those in the middle who realize that both of these viewpoints have some validity, but find themselves in the quandary of who and what to believe. You would think that after two thousand years the Bible would be a more definitive book and not one that stirs up such controversy—especially since it is considered to be a holy book. The problem is that the Bible has its flaws that have never been fixed and from all indications never will be. It is simply not a very reliable book and has many inconsistencies throughout its pages. Now, I'm sure that I will be blasted by Christian and Judaic fundamentalists who believe I am being blasphemous, but the facts are clear for all to see.

One of the big problems that arise is that the Bible is one of the few books that have survived to give us any sort of indication of humankind's history in that part of the world. If you look at the Bible as a history book, it may still have flaws, but it also has some confirmed truths and is more trustworthy. As a religious book recounting many stories of heroes and interactions with God, and putting forth religious philosophies, it can not only be inconsistent and illogical, but can also put forth falsehoods about God and, in my humble opinion, Jesus Christ.

Here we are in the twenty-first century—more learned, more literate, more scientific and, hopefully, more logical because of these qualities and yet the Bible is still a tremendous influence on our society. Some may say that just proves the holiness of the Bible, as it has influenced society for almost two thousand years, but that is not really a logical argument. The fact is that religion has perpetuated its holiness over that time, and if there is any one area of human endeavor that is most controversial it certainly has to be religion.

The various religions of the world have always been steeped in controversy and have caused more wars, conflict, and killing among humankind than any other human endeavor. Some religions are more soft-sell, like the Eastern religions of Buddhism, Hinduism, and in truth, Judaism (which is just trying to survive). Christianity and Islam have always taken the initiative and the position to be hard-sell—they will try to convert anyone, anywhere, at any time.

In the Middle Ages and even into the Renaissance the Catholic Church reigned supreme. With their various crusades and inquisitions, they took a hard line toward any who didn't follow their faith. They killed literally hundreds of thousands in their various purges against the followers of Islam, paganism, and Gnosticism. Islam has changed dramatically in the present day. At one time it was one of the most tolerant religions on earth, as evidenced by the great leader Saladin giving mercy to Crusaders and signing treaties that allowed Christian pilgrims to worship in Jerusalem in complete safety. Nowadays, although it is still basically a tolerant religion, it is being more influenced by radical clerics and extremists, to the point where that tolerance is quickly fading into the sunset.

Islam is the fastest-growing religion on earth right now, and Muslims are very adamant about converting any and all they can—even to the point where extreme conservative branches of the religion utilize terrorism as a means to get rid of those in their way. I have met and interacted with many followers of Islam, and I find them to be a loving, kind, and friendly people. I have many friends in Egypt and Turkey and other parts of the world who are Muslim,

and I love them very much. I find that they are as horrified
at terrorism as I am. Unfortunately, all of this terrorism by
extremists is putting a black eye on the world of Islam and
the religion in general, and I consider it a great tragedy.

Even though Jesus survived his crucifixion and eventually went to France, he had nothing to do with the formation of the Bible. He did want his words written down
for posterity, but he never really thought about making
a book with the scope of the Bible as we know it today.
According to some scholars, Magdalene might have had
more influence in that area than Jesus, although she
never got directly involved with it either. Mary had no
influence on the Bible or even the formation of the early
Christian Church, but she certainly became a focal point
of the Catholic Church several centuries later. As I have
stated previously, the Bible came into being and eventually evolved out of the infighting of the different factions
of early Christianity. You basically had the factions of the
followers of Peter and Paul (Pauline Christianity) against
the Jewish Christians headed by James (Jesus's brother),

and then you also had the Gnostic influence, with various Gnostics in both camps. It wasn't until the late fourth century and early fifth century that the basic structure of the Catholic Bible took place, and it has been honed and polished ever since.

It all started with the Council of Nicaea in 325 C.E. The Roman emperor Constantine called the council to try and get unanimity in the Christian religion, which had just been adopted as the state religion of Rome. Early Christianity was really not organized under one banner. You had many churches in different areas that belonged to different "divisions" of Christianity, and each had its own favored Christian writings. You had the Armenian, Assyrian Church of the East, Byzantine, Coptic, Eastern Orthodox, Ethiopian, Oriental Orthodox, and Syrian, to name just the main ones. All had different slants on how the Christian religion should be and how it should be run. Emperor Constantine wanted to put an end to that and put them all under one roof, which evolved to be the Catholic Church.

I think author and history professor Richard Carrier puts forth the best what it was like in the opening paragraph of his essay "The Formation of the New Testament Canon," which follows:

> Contrary to common belief, there was never a one-time, truly universal decision as to which books should be included in the Bible. It took over a century of the proliferation of numerous writings before anyone even bothered to start picking and choosing, and then it was largely a cumulative, individual and happenstance event, guided by chance and prejudice more than objective and scholarly research, until priests and academics began pronouncing what was authoritative and holy, and even they were not unanimous. Every church had its favored books, and since there was nothing like a clearly-defined orthodoxy until the fourth century, there were in fact many simultaneous literary traditions. The illusion that it was otherwise is created by the fact that the church that came out on top simply preserved texts in its favor and destroyed or let vanish opposing documents. Hence what we call "orthodoxy" is simply "the church that won."

After much infighting for about three hundred years, it was the faction that followed Paul's writings (Pauline Christianity) that won. They didn't win without a fight, however. That is evidenced by the many Judaic traditions that were incorporated into the Church, such as: adaptation of synagogue liturgical worship, prayer, use of Sacred Scripture, a priesthood, a religious calendar commemorating on certain days each year certain events and/or beliefs, use of music in worship, giving material support to the religious leadership, use of incense in worship and ceremonies, and practices such as fasting, almsgiving, and baptism. Scholars also say that the Greco-Roman influence started the practice of genuflection because pagan Roman priests called pontiffs (another influence) did so in front of the statues of their gods.

Some Gnostics had some influence, and Marcion of Sinope (considered by some to be a Gnostic, while others insist he wasn't) also had great influence, if in no other way than that Gnostic viewpoints were rejected in carving out church canon. Marcion put forth that the Old Testament should not be accepted as canon or put in the Bible, and he was a dualist like many of the Gnostics—believing that the God of the Old Testament was evil and that the God of the New Testament was the true God of love. He also put forth that only a "revised" Gospel of Luke, called the Gospel of Marcion, and the ten Epistles of Paul should be in the Christian Bible. Marcion argued that Christianity should be solely based on Christian love. He even went so far as to say that Christ's mission was to overthrow the Demiurge ("evil god")—the fickle, cruel, despotic God of the Old Testament—and replace him with the supreme God of love that Jesus revealed. He was excommunicated in 144 C.E. as a heretic, although his writings certainly had a profound effect on the canon of Christianity. He eventually formed his own religion, which was called Marcionism. This lasted for only a few centuries and then died out.

Probably the most influential Gnostic was Valentinus, who was almost elected pope in or about 143 C.E. Eventually, however, he broke from the Church to pursue his Gnostic writings. His followers were called Valentinians and his school of Gnosticism became very famous. In general, Gnostics were persecuted for their beliefs because they were felt to undermine the political as well as religious norm. Many ancient Gnostics didn't emphasize Christ as

God, although many recognized his divinity as a prophet or messenger from God, and that along with their belief in duality created the greatest schism. Modern Gnosticism has modified duality, believing that man himself has perpetuated and created the evil in the world and that God is all-loving and merciful.

Hundreds of years later, Rome recognized Pauline Christianity as their church and the battle was ended. It took almost another hundred years for the Bible to take the basic form we have today, as exclusion and indecision delayed a definitive book. We see how confusing and convoluted these writings became, especially as related to getting rid of most of the writings about women—unless they portrayed women in a negative light. The Church did include the Old Testament writings, which included the stories of Ruth, Esther, and Deborah. Though Esther does save her people, there is strangely no mention of her relationship to God. Some of these books seem to be add-ons or just inserted to make a point.

Nevertheless, truth will seek its way to the light and grow no matter how long it takes. It's like one time in arid Arizona I saw a flower blooming out of a crack among tons of rock. Like truth, I thought, it will find its way out no matter what the obstacles may be. That's why we live in an exciting time.

The fourth century C.E. was perhaps the most important as far as defining what we know as Christianity today. One of the major topics discussed at the Council of Nicaea in 325 was Arianism. Arianism was a theology taught by the Church theologian Arius, who had a school in the city of Alexandria in Egypt. The basic concept of Arianism was that Jesus was not a part of God, but a creation of God, who was divine. Notice here how the premise of whether or not Jesus was God on earth comes up time and again in the early Church. Arianism was basically a watered down viewpoint of the early Jewish Christians who believed Christ was a divine prophet and teacher, but not God. At the Council of Nicaea, Arianism was a topic of heated discussion, and the opponents of Arianism were led and influenced by Bishop Athanasius of Alexandria. Athanasius fought against Arianism all his life. He was exiled at least a half dozen times and brought back into favor a like number of times, depending on the views of the Roman emperor who was in power at the time. Constantine died in 337, twelve years after the Council of Nicaea, and was followed by his son, who was followed by another emperor, and on and on it went. As is evident in the results of the Council of Nicaea, which condemned Arius and Arianism, Constantine was on Bishop Athanasius's side. Out of the Council of Nicaea came the Nicene Creed, which forever made as canon the Church belief that Christ is God and a part of the Holy Trinity.

The traditions of the Roman Empire died hard though, and many of the succeeding emperors (including Constantine's son) were still waffling between paganism and Christianity. Consequently, even though Arianism was condemned by the Church as heretical, it continued to flourish. It was still taught throughout various parts of the Roman Empire for several hundred years after its condemnation at Nicaea.

Athanasius was also instrumental in defining what books would be included in the initial Christian Bible. He wrote his own personal list of what books should be included, and the Church did indeed follow that list. They adopted the listed books as canon. The debate on what books should have been included and what books should have been excluded started at Nicaea, but didn't end until the early fifth century, when the initial Bible was more or less formalized. I say "more or less" because the Church simply burned or disposed of offending writings and confined their holy writings to those that were on the list. Just as the world lost a great deal of precious writings when the Library of Alexandria was burned by conquerors, so the world also lost innumerable precious writings that were destroyed by the early Christian church. As many have said over the ages, "History is written by the winners," but it is really humankind who has lost. We can never get back the vast tomes of writings and books of wisdom and history because they were destroyed by these "winners."

Regardless of this chaotic backdrop, history is coming in to validate or try to validate what is truth and what is false. With new discoveries come new knowledge and truth. That is the way it has always been. After over three hundred years of infighting and maneuvering for power by hundreds of men who each had his own agenda, a consensus was finally reached. It doesn't make the consensus right, but the "winners" could now force their will and agenda on the world in general. People like Athanasius, who had argued that his list of twenty-seven books—and only them—make up the Bible, could now impart their beliefs and will on the masses. Over forty books and innumerable writings were now tossed aside on the scrap heap as either apocryphal or heretical. They would no longer have much influence as far as the Church was concerned, and all were basically ignored or destroyed. Basically, the early Church took the standpoint that the books included in their Bible were the only truth, and they quickly gained the money and power to enforce it through guilt, fear, intimidation and, if necessary, even violence.

I am constantly amazed that humankind has always equated having power to having truth and/or "being right." Having power does not make you an expert on truth, nor does it even give you the real truth, for truth comes from God. It does allow you, however, to manipulate truth and to enforce whatever truth you believe on others. A clear example of this is Hitler. He enforced his truth and agenda on millions of people with the power of his armies. Humankind has always had its despots, tyrants, and authoritive figures who have ruled, manipulated, and enforced their perceived truths and will on others—be it by an individual, government, or religion. In many cases, they did it quite successfully, and they all had the common denominator of power. Power is a highly prized commodity for gaining wealth and control, but it invariably is misused and abused because of human emotions and the makeup of humankind. There is ample evidence that the Catholic Church was no exception as massive corruption ran rampant in the Church throughout the Middle Ages and into the Renaissance. This led to the uprising and schism in the Church known as the Reformation.

What most people fail to realize or are unaware of is the fact that Jesus was a rebel who fought against the concept of power. He knew it was only a transient and fleeting commodity that was indigenous to this earth plane of existence. He knew that the reality is the Other Side and that it is eternal. With all the dissention and chaos that exists on earth even to this day, we'll hopefully come to common ground and spiritually believe a message of truth. The Bible was and is made up largely by fallible men and interpreted by fallible men (regardless of the fact that the Catholic Church believes the pope to be infallible). The theme of Jesus's life, however, still seems to thread through as well as his love of Magdalene, his mother, his siblings, apostles, and humankind. It still survives when you cut away all of the excess fat. His words still ring the truth loudly, but many times they have unfortunately been manipulated and interpreted to bring guilt, fear, control, and ultimately used to gain more power. I'm sure he never ever wanted his words to be used to advance religious agendas. He only wanted the people to know the truth about God and the Kingdom of Heaven.

I'm optimistic that people, who as our Lord says have eyes to see and ears to hear, will cut through all the morass of words and various dogmas and find their own spiritual truth. Not to be glib, but it seems that a few apostles as well as Mary, Jesus, and Magdalene were just putting out the philosophy of "can't we all just get along." Their approach was to keep it simple and honor God and the messenger who brought us this loving God that made everyone equal. Can't we just realize God made and loves each and every one of us and stop using the message of Jesus as a weapon to create power, control, and bigotry? Organized religions keep messing up the works with their penchant for power, wealth, and control. They constantly have their theologians debate this and that, thinking in their massive egos, and their ivory towers of power that they are the only ones who have and can dispense truth. It is hypocrisy in its finest hour, and as the Bible points out many times, Jesus hated hypocrites.

It really boils down to common sense. If a Christian evangelical preacher gives a sermon on God's love for us all and then turns around and gives a sermon damning homosexuals as the vilest of the vile who will surely go to hell, then he completely misses the point of the makeup of God and the message of Jesus. Christ said, "Do not judge, lest ye be judged." God cannot love everybody and then turn around and condemn or destroy them. And for what? Sexual practices? I think God is certainly above such pettiness.

Why do you think organized religions have different teachings, rules, and regulations (dogma) and that they vary so much? If you think it's because they are trying to keep their followers from "sinning," you only have a partial truth or can only see the tip of the iceberg. Dogma is nothing more than cultural teaching and moral traditions that have been handed down through generations. Morality is geographical and cultural in nature. Tribes in the Amazon have no problem with women showing their breasts, while many other areas consider it to be a sin or morally degenerate. Certainly, there are the biggies of human behavior, such as murder and theft, that are condemned in almost every culture. From there on, however, cultural traditions can vary widely and so can their taboos. Organized religions then put these taboos in their religious writings such as the Bible, Koran, Torah, etc., and in the specific dogmas of their religions. It is interesting to note that no other area of human behavior has the attention of this dogma more than sexual practices and human sexuality. It seems as if organized religion went out of its way to make sure sex was its main entrée as it relates to moral practices.

In my opinion, they have their priorities all mixed up. Place the emphasis on teaching people to be kind, loving, and considerate to their fellow human beings first and foremost. If human beings were schooled more in the Golden Rule then you just might find that sexual crimes, divorce, and adulterous behavior would take a sharp dip in their rates of occurrence. To change the world's propensity for war and conflict to one of peace and goodwill is not going to be done by monitoring sexual behavior. One must take a higher road to not only religious tolerance, but racial and ethnic tolerance. The higher road entails showing respect for human life and easing the suffering of millions. In other words, religion should focus on teaching spirituality rather than concentrating on the morality issues of such mundane things as human sexuality.

Think about it for a moment. Put yourself in God's shoes. Would you really care if two humans had sex out of wedlock or were the same gender? The seeking of earthly pleasure is only wrong if it is done with malicious intent to hurt someone else. Even then, the act is not as important as the intent behind the act. I have always said that the key to spirituality is not only love, but to live your life with good intentions. If I am God, I am not going to care whether or not you have kinky sex, but I will care if you maliciously try to hurt someone in any way with your actions and deeds. If you spread false rumors to get a promotion, lie or cheat someone to get ahead or to get wealth or power, intentionally hurt someone out of jealousy, anger, or because that person is a different color or practices a different religion or just looks different, then if I am God

I will care. Will God care if you eat certain foods, drink certain beverages, bow down to pray or stand up to pray or don't pray at all? Will God care if you go to church, or choose not to go to church, or choose to practice a certain religion instead of another? I think you get the point. God loves us all and only wants us to be happy. It's as simple as that. God doesn't care about what religion you practice or whether or not you practice any religion at all, as long as it makes you happy and more spiritual. God doesn't care about whether you are celibate or promiscuous, or whether you are homosexual or heterosexual. If your actions make you happier and more spiritual, God is all for it—as long as you don't harm anyone else with malicious intent.

God loves all of His/Her creations, and that love will not allow any part of creation to be destroyed. God is perfect and all-loving, and even that which we may consider to be evil is still loved by God. This is called "unconditional love," and God has it for all of what we may call His/Her children—which includes us. Does God love a sinner any less than a good person? Of course not, for God would then be imperfect and not have an unconditional love for creation. One may then ask the obviously human question, "If God loves a sinner as much as us, what is the point in being good?" The person who is honestly trying to be the best person he or she can be and to be good in all thoughts, actions, and deeds is actually walking the path to Godliness. In doing good works, you become more like God and bring yourself closer to God. God is forever and omnipotently close to everyone, but those who gain in spirituality by living a good life become a reflection of God in human form. God then becomes a smile, a kindness done for another, a helping hand in time of need, a love that shines outwardly through a human soul to embrace all that it comes in contact with. Some say God is dead or doesn't exist because there is no tangible proof of God's existence. That is pure folly, for every day we see the manifestation of God in the millions of people who shine with spirituality in doing good works.

Life on this earth is transient, temporary, and can end in a blink of an eye. Life in the reality of creation, which is the Other Side, is eternal and filled with eternal happiness. Life on earth is nothing more than the curriculum of God's school to teach us spirituality. To gain the eternal bliss of the Other Side and all its glory permanently, we must learn in this school called earth all of the aspects of true spirituality, and by doing so we will no longer have to return to this plane of negativity. We can, as Jesus said, "reside in the Kingdom of God" forever and ever.

In Judaism there was always a prophet anointed by God to help serve and guide the people. There were many throughout the years, including Jonah, Daniel, Ezekiel, Elijah, Deborah, Jeremiah, Amos, and Isaiah, to name just a few. Tragically, their prophecies concerned the bad things that would happen to the people of Israel if they didn't keep to their faith. According to some biblical scholars, there are also prophecies concerning the Savior or Messiah who would come into the world to save them from bondage and suffering and create world peace. Christian scholars believe these prophecies about the Savior directly relate to Jesus and his life and hence have declared him the Messiah that it was foretold would come. Naturally, Jewish scholars disagree. If they didn't, there would be no Judaic faith today, for the Judaic faith still believes their Messiah was not Jesus and has yet to come.

Scholars who are more objective say that biblical prophecies concerning a savior or messiah are at best obscure and at worst completely misinterpreted or nonexistent. Ancient prophecy, for the most part, is steeped in obscurity. The Greek oracle at Delphi spoke in obscure language or riddles that could be interpreted in many different ways. If you read some of the supposed prophecies in the Old Testament, you'll see that many of them are very opaque in nature and can have hidden meanings and can also be interpreted in different ways. It is almost as if ancient prophets could not or would not speak in a direct manner. This, of course, kept them in power as prophets, because most of the ancient peoples of the world considered their God or Gods to be unknowable. Only the words of God as spoken through their prophets kept them in touch with the Almighty. So what if what these prophets said didn't make sense? God was so mighty and unknowable that only these anointed prophets could contact Him and receive His word and only they could interpret for the people what God said. These prophets had power and the respect and adoration of the people and could control kings; but many times they quarreled within their ranks, went naked, ate scrolls, were very zealous, and if viewed today by psychiatrists would be considered mentally ill. I'm not being discriminatory, but their main mission in life always seemed to be very political and one of controlling the people. Jesus, on the other hand, was more for the individual man and woman. He constantly tried to give the message to take care of your own individual spirituality rather than cater to the state or government. And that's what Jesus and Magdalene kept teaching throughout their lives.

Tragically, even the disciples got caught up in the politics of deciding who the chosen leader of the apostles was and who was the closest to Jesus. They would sometimes bicker over these issues as they traveled with Jesus in his public life, and it became an even bigger issue after Jesus left them. Magdalene got caught up in this a little bit as she was obviously Jesus's favorite, but she basically tried to stay out of their petty quarrels and concentrated on taking the notes that show up in her gospel.

In the book *The Gospel of Mary of Magdala* by noted author Karen L. King, King points out that numerous early Christian works are ascribed to Peter, including the canonical letters of I and 2 Peter, the Gospel of Peter, the Letter of Peter to Philip, the Apocalypse of Peter, the Kerygama Petri, and the Acts of Peter. She then states, "But while this literature consistently takes Peter as a guarantor of apostolic authority and paints him in positive terms, he remains theologically elusive, in part because he is used to authorize conflicting theological positions." This certainly validates that history is written by not only the "winners," but the ones who were intellectual enough in that time to write down their views to suit their own religious agenda. King goes on to say, "While Irenaeus [a powerful bishop of the early Christian church who had great influence on what gospels were canonized] uses Peter as a witness to the physical reality of Jesus' incarnation, the 'Apocalypse of Peter' has him receive a revelation from the Savior that rejects the incarnation and affirms that Jesus only *seemed* to have a body." Here we have Peter evidently recanting on seeing Christ after the crucifixion in a physical body as is related in several of the other canonized gospels. King then says in her book, "After Mary of Magdala and other unnamed women meet the angel at the tomb and flee in fear, Peter along with Andrew and Levi go out fishing."

The point I'm trying to make here is that Peter is looked on by most people as the "first pope," the leader of the apostles, and the acknowledged head of the early Church at that time. In truth it seems that image was put forth by the early Church, and scholars pretty much agree that Peter was an ambiguous figure. The early Church had a problem and that problem was Mary Magdalene and her relationship with Jesus. We find many writings that support the position that Magdalene was not only "the apostle that Jesus loved the most," but also very respected for her understanding of Jesus's teachings. She was probably the real leader of the apostles. The leaders of the early Church could not accept a woman as one of the apostles, let alone the leader of them. They then elevated Peter to that position, even though it was known that he was a hothead and caused a lot of dissension among the apostles. They edited the necessary books to substantiate Peter's elevation and also made sure that Magdalene was suppressed.

Karen King goes on to say, "After the second century, Peter continued to have a long and illustrious afterlife in legend, art, and ecclesiastical politics as the preeminent apostle of Christian faith, the co-founder of the Roman church, and the apostolic guarantor for papal authority." Although the Church elevated Peter's status, the view of Peter held by others who knew him was not one of such high esteem. Levi (Matthew) says that Peter had a temper and caused discord by being impetuous. In the Gospel of Mary, Peter is shown to be an ignorant hothead and a troublemaker. Jesus called Peter "Satan" in Mark (8:31–33), and Jesus had to save Peter from drowning in the Gospel of Matthew (14:29–31) because of his lack of faith. We can also see that Peter was very fearful, as is illustrated by his denying Christ three times, and that is related in all the canonical gospels. The Gospel of Mark paints a picture of Peter as an unreliable blusterer. Jesus seemed to admonish Peter a lot, e.g., in the garden at Gethsemane, where Peter fell asleep. He was also admonished at this location for cutting off a servant's ear with his sword (at least he showed some courage there). In the Gospel of Mark he tells Jesus he was wrong about the crucifixion and is called Satan. In the gospel of John he refuses to have Jesus wash his feet and raises the ire of Jesus. The Gospel of the Nazarenes (not canonized) was not convinced of his character and said the final judgment of Peter could be condensed into: "denied and swore and damned himself." Even Paul had problems with Peter, when he said he was a hypocrite and modified his behavior depending upon his audience.

Many early religious writings paint Peter as hot tempered, hypocritical, bold and yet fearful, and somewhat dumb, because he didn't always understand Christ's teachings or what was going on.

The early Church negated all of this, however, and inserted passages where it was thought necessary to give a better picture of Peter. The Bible has Paul acknowledging Peter as a leader in the Jerusalem church and also has Paul accepting Peter in the role of "apostle to the circumcised." Through the Gospel of Luke and the Acts of the Apostles, Peter's image is upgraded by calling him the leader of the apostles, a miracle worker, and a bold evangelist. The Gospel of Luke also tries to suppress Magdalene's importance by referring to the seven demons within her that were cast out and portraying her as a financial supporter of Jesus's ministry. According to Karen King, scholars suspect these two tidbits of data as perhaps an obvious attempt to reduce Magdalene's (and all women's, for that matter) importance and put her in a subservient role.

In contrast, early writings such as the Gospel of Thomas, the First Apocalypse of James, the Dialogue of the Savior, the Sophia of Jesus Christ, the Gospel of Philip, the Pistis Sophia, and the Gospel of Mary all portray Mag-dalene as a prominent disciple of Jesus. Note also that none of these writings were canonized.

Karen King says, "Peter appears solely in his role as ignorant hothead. His challenge to Magdalene presents him as a jealous man who cannot see past the weakness of the flesh to discern spiritual truth." I see Magdalene's reduced importance as partly Peter's fault, but more the writers, who wanted a male leader rather than a female. A female leader would have been against the presiding laws of the Old Testament, which belittled women. The Church politics that were ruled by men certainly wanted to get rid of this woman, whom Jesus loved more than the other disciples.

Again, in *The Gospel of Mary of Magdala*, King states, "Early Christian gospel traditions generally accord Mary of Magdala a prominent position among the followers of Jesus." She then goes on to say, "She is one of the main speakers in several first and second century texts recording dialogues of Jesus with his disciples after the resurrection." As we have discussed earlier, his resurrection was a sham to help cover his escape and these dialogues were with the still-living Jesus. Modern scholars are now convinced that Magdalene was much closer to Jesus than most thought or portrayed her to be. Without fanfare, she is now generally acknowledged by true theologians to be the "apostle to the apostles," which she wholeheartedly deserves. There is ongoing research that is delving into her life more and more.

The story of Jesus as put forth by the Christian faith has had its roots for two thousand years in the biblical account of the four canonized gospels. The Catholic Church has beaten back all challengers to its version of the truth, and the Protestant branch of Christianity has gone along for the ride. This just shows that Christianity in general is a great example of what propaganda can do to the general populace. Christianity's hold on its version of the truth is still strong, however, but it is getting more tenuous because of the bravery of several authors and—of all things—a movie director.

Except for the occasional scholars who were effectively silenced by the Church by labeling them heretics or crazy zealots, the Christian version of the truth about Jesus was rarely challenged. One of the main reasons it lasted for so long was the lack of technology. As humankind has made advances in technology and become more learned, it has become easier to do research. Advancement in the speed of communications now allows scholars, researchers, and scientists to collaborate with one another more effectively. In this new age of technology, unwanted publicity can become a nightmare to control, and organized religions cannot exert control over the masses like they once did. The masses are now more educated and can express their opinions with more freedom. Dissenters can no longer be tortured or killed by burning them at the stake. A new age has dawned, and organized religions will be hard-pressed to keep their archaic beliefs unscathed and intact. With the instant communications that we now have, no one can stop truth from coming out.

The recent upsurge in public interest is probably directly related to the massive success of Dan Brown's novel *The Da Vinci Code,* which was published in 2003 and has sold over 60 million copies and still counting as of 2006. In truth, though, it really started with an earlier book from which Dan Brown got the idea for his novel.

The book *Holy Blood, Holy Grail* by authors Michael Baigent, Richard Leigh, and Henry Lincoln was published in 1982. Besides creating an immediate controversy, it became an international bestseller. Its premise was that Jesus and Mary Magdalene were married, had one or more children, and their bloodline survives today. The book was banned by the Church and was later found to be based on questionable facts that were supposedly part of a hoax perpetuated by a French con man named Pierre Plantard. The authors had done extensive research on the book for over fifteen years and contend it was based on hypothesis. Regardless of whether or not some of their facts were false, many facts in the book were true. Scholars and historians, however, blasted the book because it was based partly on information that was part of an apparent hoax.

I give kudos to these three authors for not only their courage in writing the book but also for their hypothesis. They have been maligned and their reputations have suffered greatly because of the hoax scandal, but I believe most of what they have written to be true. Their subsequent book, *The Messianic Legacy*, was also a bestseller but was similarly received by critics as untruthful. What I find interesting is that one of the main thrusts of their books is the mystery of Rennes-le-Château—the same Rennes-le-Château area in which Francine reports that Jesus, Mary, and Magdalene settled so many years ago. Coincidence? I doubt it. To give a summary of the Rennes-le-Château mystery, there was a poor Catholic priest who took over the parish of Rennes-le-Château in the latter part of the nineteenth century. He supposedly found documents in a hollow pillar in the small church there and, immediately after informing his bishop of his discovery, became very wealthy. He then renovated the parish church and built a tower to Mary Magdalene with the newfound wealth. Speculation says he found a treasure or a secret that the Church then paid him to keep silent on. The renovation of the church is bizarre in nature, and the whole mystery has been linked to conspiracy theories. There is also the premise believed by many that it was a gigantic story made up by a local innkeeper to increase business. You can always get more information on this mystery by doing a little research.

I also want to give some kudos to Martin Scorsese, who directed the 1988 film *The Last Temptation of Christ*. It was a brave endeavor and although somewhat bizarre in places, it can be a shocking film for conservative Christians and will have them shouting "foul" from now until doomsday. I found the premise most interesting: that Jesus was married to Mary Magdalene in a type of dream sequence. I will not even attempt to summarize this film, but you can get it to view at home. It is somewhat weird, so beware.

God bless these brave individuals and all those who speak out against oppression and untruths, for without them the world would be even more oppressed than it is now. I certainly don't want to give the impression that I am against any religion or belief, because I have always been a champion for religious tolerance and freedom. I am, however, also against perpetuating hypocrisy, lies, and blatant distortions of the truth—especially when it comes to God and religion, which affects us all.

CHAPTER 7

A Woman for the Ages

FTER THE DEATH of Mary, Jesus and Magdalene carried on with their mission of teaching and healing. It was hard for both of them because Mary was such an important part of their lives. Both were healthy and strong, though, and that was due in large part to Mary. Mary knew a lot about cures and natural early medicine and handed that knowledge down to both of them. The one thing that I myself regret is that out of all the things that I learned from my psychic grandmother, I didn't absorb more of her superb holistic knowledge. Her innate learning and infused knowing about what poultice should be used was phenomenal. Her cupboards were filled with valerian root, dragon's blood, Saint-John's-wort, and so many others that I can't remember. She also had a great devotion to Mary, saying she was a blessing from God. She was the first one to tell me, when I was around ten, that Magdalene was never a bad woman.

This didn't begin to resonate with me until I was older and began to research. We even see that in Christianity, depending on what you read or what Christian sect is putting out the information, that Mary is either called "The Mother of God" or "The Mother of Jesus." If Jesus was God, then why did he always refer to his Father in heaven and always say the Kingdom of God rather than refer to it as "his" kingdom? As is well known to scholars and researchers, there is a lot of disagreement between the different factions of Christianity as to whether or not Jesus is God or the son of God. Religious interpretation is so exhausting and tedious, so why can't we just believe what we wish to believe? If you look closely at what the Bible says, you'll see that he becomes the son of man and God, but is never referred to as God. But live and let live.

Many of the apocryphal and Gnostic writings, as well

as newly found writings like the Gospel of Mary and the Gospel of Judas, have an advantage as far as scholars and historians are concerned in that they are not included in the Bible. This means they are less likely to have been edited by the early Church and thus may give us a clearer picture of what was going on in the time they were written. These writings are more affiliated with the "losers" and thus may be more accurate. They will at least give us a picture of the opposite side of the coin. Scholars and scientists will always have the usual detractors who will question authenticity and doubt who actually wrote some of these writings. This is good, though, because it gives us a verification system against fake and fraudulent items. Much of what is unearthed cannot really be proven to be genuine one way or the other. For example, if someone thought they'd found the tomb of Jesus or Magdalene, what DNA would we have to prove it was them? Many times scholars only have logical and partial historical or archaeological knowledge to go on and try to piece those clues together. They don't always have enough knowledge to categorically prove they are right.

Magdalene's gospel tells us much about how she knew

Jesus, and it fits perfectly with his type of dialogue. You can tell when writing has changed hands: the whole cadence changes, the wording is different, and the teachings have a different style. Her Gospel of Mary is pure to Jesus's type of teaching and the style by which he gave his knowledge. Sure, she was helped by Mary and Jesus, but Mary, being his mother, would have related what he said in perfect order. He warned against falseness in belief and strongly advocated keeping his simple teachings pure for following the path of good deeds and moral ethics. Magdalene and Mary always imparted the love of self and your fellow man.

We can see this in the Gospel of Mary where it relates Jesus's words when he talks to his disciples just before they are to go out into the world with his message:

> Be of good courage, and if you are discouraged, still take courage against the various forms of nature. He who has ears to hear let him hear. Take heed, lest anyone lead you astray with the words, "Lo here!" or "Lo there!" for the Son of Man is within you.

Notice how he now calls himself the Son of Man and later he says:

Go therefore, and preach the Gospel of the Kingdom. I have left no commandment but what I have commanded you, and I have given you no law as the lawgiver did, lest you be bound by it.

Far-seeing as he was, he wanted to impart to Magdalene that he wanted no rules except the few he had given. He probably knew that his words would get misinterpreted and those who came after him wouldn't take his words for what they meant in simple terms. He somehow knew that they would interpret them to fit their own agenda and that of course is exactly what happened.

Jesus lived many years after his mother died, and trained the children and talked to small "student" groups. He left the main teachings, however, to Magdalene. I'm sure this was not out of fear of discovery, but more to let people know of her position as not only his wife and the mother of his children, but the driving force behind his teachings. He never once refers to church in Mary's gospel, but again speaks more to keep his teachings pure.

On the website Magdalene.org, under their section on perspectives, they have a good article on "The Traditional Christian Perspective." They give a good overview of the controversies that have surrounded Mary Magdalene. They state that in the early Middle Ages her reputation as a repentant sinner was solidified. They go on to say that even though the timeline is disputed, around the eleventh century she was lauded as a preacher and healer (the latter role she learned from Mary and continued the practice after Mary's death). They also state that she went to Gaul (France) and others were with her. They don't mention Jesus, but only say that she didn't go alone. They go on to state that the "traditional Christian view" of her being a repentant sinner remained static until 1969, when the Catholic Church quietly removed all references to her as a penitent sinner and began to refer to her as a disciple. Non-Catholic Christians still hold various beliefs about Magdalene. Their beliefs range from Magdalene being married to Jesus to the extreme view that she was a redeemed "prostitute." I'm sure this dispute will go on forever, but there now is so much revelation and historical background on Magdalene that it seems to me to be almost indisputable that she was never a prostitute. This only validates the real love and reverence they have for her in France—more than any other state or country.

Many ministries that help young women now carry her name—whether they are for unwed mothers, the homeless, or women with addiction problems (although this still seems to be in the theme of a repentant sinner). This must make her happy that, like Jesus, she is finally coming into her own as a healer and saver of people—her mission in life. Even if it took two thousand years, there is no sense of time on the Other Side. And really, what does it matter as long as her long-overdue respect is finally here?

A group of scholars (the most noted being Elaine Pagels and Ann Graham Brock) suggests that Magdalene was a leader of the early Church and was in all probability the heretofore unidentified "beloved disciple" to which the fourth canonized Gospel of John has been ascribed. This theory is certainly not new, and new research by some biblical scholars now seems to indicate that Magdalene is indeed the "beloved disciple" and the "disciple that Jesus loved the most." Scholars also point out that Magdalene could very well have been an early leader of a faction of Christianity, as she is portrayed as a leader in writings from which formal leadership roles are absent. This would put her in opposition and conflict with Peter and Paul because they wanted a patriarchal leadership, and as we all know their viewpoint was the one adopted. I believe the main reason for this was because Magdalene was so devoted to Jesus and really didn't want to get into the politics of starting a church. She just wanted to convey Christ's teachings simplistically. Any leadership role she played would have ended with their escape and the sending of the disciples out into the world as apostles. You might say that both Jesus and Magdalene washed their hands of the politics in the forming of the early Christian Church and just concentrated on teaching. They probably knew the Church would turn into a chaotic mess.

For those who are seriously interested in learning more about these early power struggles, I highly recommend that you read Elaine Pagels's *Beyond Belief: The Secret Gospel of Thomas* and Ann Graham Brock's *Mary Magdalene, The First Apostle: The Struggle for Authority*. You also might be interested in Karen L. King's *The Gospel of Mary Magdala*. Brock's book is very scholarly, with many footnotes, but has a lot of good information on power struggles in the early Church. Pagels's book is just a classic.

These early gospels of Mary, Thomas, and Philip, which were not canonized by the early Church, seem to hold more truth than first thought. This truth is being discussed as new information is coming more and more to light. More and more writers today have come forward with claims that Magdalene was not only the wife of Jesus, but also a leader of the early Christian movement and church. Whether it is historical, or scientific, or even pure speculation, this idea is being brought more into the mainstream by the researchers of these subjects.

As stated earlier, after Mary's death Jesus and Magdalene carried on, but they found themselves staying closer and closer to home. As time went on, Jesus was more of an absentee teacher, with Magdalene in the foreground. Magdalene started having real visions from Mary, and she also found that her healing prowess was becoming more and more successful. People from the surrounding areas would bring their sick to Magdalene and she would heal them.

The old, the infirm, the crippled, and even the terminal were constantly being brought to her. Jesus would still heal at times, but he too was getting older and felt that his time was near. Magdalene, as sanctified as she was, dreaded the day when she would be alone. Sure, she had children and the community, but the two main backups of Mary and Jesus would be gone and all would be left to her. No matter how strong one might be, this is a frightening situation to be in.

I remember how cast adrift I felt when my psychic grandmother died. Even though she had given me so much at that time in the 1950s, there was no one left who was psychic or understood how I felt. Sure, my father encouraged me, but I had no one to go to who could relate to what I saw or felt. So, in some strange and foreign way, I can empathize with Magdalene.

The apostles would randomly find their way to her, but always in secrecy. The gospels of Thomas and Philip show they had conversations with her, as did John, although most of them were very patriarchal in nature. The Gospel of Philip keeps reiterating that Magdalene was definitely closer to Jesus than any other disciple. He also goes on to call her *koinonos*—a Greek term meaning "lover," "companion," or "partner." Their relationship as described in these writings depicts Mary Magdalene as understanding Jesus and his teachings much more than the rest of the disciples. This perhaps instilled the jealousy that is evident with some of the disciples (principally Peter).

Another important fact that I was aware of years ago came out in the book *Holy Blood, Holy Grail* and has been put forth by theorists in support of the married status of Jesus, and that is that bachelorhood was very rare for Jewish males of Jesus's time, being generally regarded as a transgression of the first mitzvah (divine commandment)—"Be fruitful and multiply." It would have been very unusual for an adult and unmarried Jewish male to travel about teaching as a rabbi. Also, Jewish men were not called "rabbi" unless they were married or a married teacher.

I'm convinced that when they found Jesus in the temple at the age of ten or twelve, he had gone through his own bar mitzvah. Think about the wedding feast of Cana. Why would Mary tell her son to turn water into wine unless she was in charge of the wedding as Jewish mothers are? No one would go into someone else's wedding and give orders.

Jesus passed peacefully away in bed at the then almost unheard of age of eighty-six. There was a golden light around him that Magdalene and Sarah and a few other witnesses saw. Esther and his two male children had left some years before and were not present at his death. It was on his deathbed where he truly said, "Father, it is finished." He had gotten Magdalene's promise to carry on and thanked her for her loyalty and love over the many years they had been together. Magdalene's heart was breaking with grief because she knew he was going to die. They had carried on after Mary's death and had been together as man and wife for over fifty years. Now she realized that except for Sarah she was going to be alone and knew she had her own cross to bear. If Jesus carried his, she would carry hers through all travails until the end of her days.

The ability to see and hear is a lonely life, especially when others do not believe you and persecute you with words that sting. She felt, though, that this was her mission now. Even if she hadn't promised Jesus at his deathbed and all through their lives kept constant, she would have made it her mission anyway. Visits by any of the original disciples were few and far between, as most all of them were dead.

To her, however, that was somewhat of a relief because they seemed to constantly argue with her over the teachings that she received from her visions of Jesus after his death.

She often had visions of Jesus and Mary in her meditative state, and she moved into a large cave after Jesus's death. She was not so spry anymore and the daily trek to the cave where she taught was hard on her. People would come to her with their maladies and she would teach almost every day. She was absolutely revered by the local people in the region and word of her teaching and healing ability spread. Her neighbors never did betray their vow to protect her identity, the same as they had kept their vow about Jesus's real identity. That might be somewhat hard to believe, but we must realize there wasn't any type of media exposure—no CNN, no newspapers. If word did leak out, it was probably thought to be madness or just a rumor. After all, hadn't many seen Jesus be crucified? This may not be the best comparison, but even today how many times did people have supposed sightings of Elvis Presley soon after he died? Many who don't want to believe their "king" is dead keep resurrecting him in their minds. In Jesus's case, however, it was true.

Jerusalem was a fairly long way from France. Many of the Roman and Judaic communities didn't pay much attention to these little conclaves of Gnostics. When the time came, though, they were the ones who were sacrificed to the lions or burned or crucified. The ruling political and religious leaders felt they were heretical to the new patriarchal Christian religion of the Roman state.

Magdalene stayed close to her group, wrote her gospel, and tried to make sure Jesus's message was kept pure for posterity. Many of the original group had died, and those who were left kept silent about Jesus, where he had lived, and certainly where he was buried. The Gnostics in the area were fearful that the Romans would grab them and wipe out their community, as Gnostics all over Rome and other areas were being persecuted and used as fodder for Rome's gladiatorial games.

Over the years, the whole region that is now known as southern France became significantly Gnostic in nature, which I'm sure was a direct result of the teachings of Jesus and Magdalene. Ten to twelve centuries later it was a stronghold for both the Knights Templar and the Cathars. It was the Knights Templar who became very wealthy after visiting the pope at that time and getting unknown information. People thought they had a big treasure and were the holders of the Holy Grail. They were, but the Holy Grail was the secret of Jesus and Magdalene being married and having children. The Knights Templar were essentially wiped out in the early fourteenth century by a collusion between the king of France and the pope. Over ten thousand Knights Templar were tortured and killed, but most died without revealing what they knew.

What I find most interesting are the Gnostics called the Cathars. The Cathars established a foothold in the south of France, and the people there embraced them wholeheartedly. They were very passive, peaceful, and highly critical of the Catholic Church and its corruption. The Church tried to roust them out of the area by sending in numerous bishops to try to bring the people back to Catholicism, and miserably failed. The pope then decided to mount a crusade against the Cathars to literally wipe them out. Here is a most interesting tidbit: this crusade was called the Albigensian Crusade because the people in southern France would often call themselves Albigensians. Notice how closely "Albigensian" resembles the last name Albengentun, which is the last name that Christ took when he settled there. The spelling could very well have been changed over the centuries, and these people could very well have been the descendents of the followers of Christ in southern France. The crusade lasted for about twenty years or so, and by the end almost all Cathars had been killed. The Cathars were also thought to have a treasure, much like the Knights Templar, and Francine says the Cathars' treasure was also the knowledge of the marriage and children of Jesus and Magdalene.

Keeping the secret of Jesus and Magdalene and their family cost many lives over the centuries with both the Knights Templar and the Cathars being literally destroyed. Even today there are many detractors about this secret, but reason and historical knowledge will be let out no matter who tries to stop them. Once the snowball of truth starts on its way down the mountain of untruths, it just gets bigger and bigger and no one can slow it down, let alone stop it. Then, in an avalanche of recognition, Jesus and Magdalene will come into their rightful place.

As is evident in the gospels of Thomas, Philip, and Mary, Magdalene fought to keep Jesus's words pure. This not only included his teachings when he was alive, but also the infused and continually inspired teachings she received in her visions of Jesus after he died. She tried to share these teachings with the other disciples when they visited, but would get notably upset if one or more of them called her a liar. It must have been very frustrating for her to have to fight these disciples, their jealousy, and their idea that women should not teach.

With all her writings, healings, and teachings, Magdalene was also getting tired. I'm sure it was somewhat lonely and depressing. She was in her seventies when Jesus died, and only her mission kept her going. Age, the raising of her children who were all gone now except for Sarah, and her intense work had and were taking their toll. The passion was still there, but the light was getting dimmer inside of her. Sarah stayed with her mother all through her life, and the other three children went off to different areas.

Magdalene lived the last twenty or so years of her life in a cave catering to those around her, but she also meditated. This probably explains the reason why many artists show her kneeling with her eyes glowing, and some early artists even show a light around her. Why would these artists give homage to a "lady of the evening" unless she was considered a saint (which she was) by the masses? Even today there are shrines dedicated to her in some of the caves in the Languedoc region. I believe we will find that in the next decade she will come into her rightful place in religion and history. Thank God.

I've said this before, but I'll say it again because reason demands it. Why would marriage and children diminish the divinity of Jesus? Somehow, religion has melded sin and sex and come out with some sort of balderdash that you have to be a virgin, and remain celibate, not be married, and not give birth to or sire children in order to be divine. Tell that to Moses, Abraham, Mohammed, and even Buddha. All were married, had sex, and had children. To this day, Catholic priests take vows of celibacy to imitate what they have always felt was the life of chastity lived by Jesus. Some divisions of the Church, like the Eastern and Oriental Orthodox churches, allow married priests, but I'm not even going to go into that. The bottom line is that it is Catholic tradition that requires vows of celibacy for the priesthood, and it has nothing to do with whether a person is divine or not.

The divinity of Jesus wouldn't be tainted by marriage and children. Even the Old Testament is filled with bringing life into the world because no matter how old you were you wanted an heir to carry on. Even if you had a lot of followers, it wasn't like having a family. In my own life I have wanted my ministers, study groups, my sons, and even my grandchildren if they so choose to carry on after I'm gone. Edgar Cayce had Hugh Lynn Cayce to carry on his work with A.R.E. (Association for Research and Enlightenment). Logically you don't spend your life giving out acquired knowledge and not want it to be carried on for the ones who come after. If it falls fallow, then in many ways the work has been in vain. My sons are both involved in my work, and this gives any mother or father a sense of completion.

In the case of Jesus and Magdalene, we don't have any information about their children other than the theorists who say they went on to found the bloodline of the Merovingian kings. Some have asked me if Jesus's bloodline is still alive. My guide Francine says no because it has been too diluted after two thousand years. Even if we did find anyone who claimed to be part of his bloodline, whose DNA would we compare it to to confirm it? That's one reason why they will never be able to prove that the Shroud of Turin is authentic, because they have no comparative blood samples or DNA from Jesus. You may even say that this whole story about Jesus and Magdalene is pure conjecture, but not with the writings and historical data and new archaeological discoveries that are being made and coming to the foreground. Researchers are diligently putting this puzzle together.

Joseph of Arimathaea, the great hero and friend and patron to Jesus and Magdalene, died anywhere from five to ten years after Mary. He was a great protector and helped them tremendously with financial support, which allowed them to live in relative privacy and comfort. Money in itself is not evil, but how you use it can be. It can be used to buy comfort, privacy, and freedom and can also be used to help the poor and needy. In that way it can be a blessing, for it goes to the greater good. In our day we see celebrities like Oprah building a school in Africa, or Montel working tirelessly for M.S., or Bill Gates giving vast amounts to fight AIDS in Africa, or Elton John giving concerts to fight AIDS. If you give, it will always come back. We call this seed money.

It is interesting to note that novels such as Dan Brown's *The Da Vinci Code* and Paul Park's *Three Marys* have become so controversial. Both say that Jesus and Magdalene were married, and granted they are novels, but both writers did a lot of research and claim that their books have a lot of facts in them. Park was unable to find a publisher for six years, lost friends, and his literary agent quit. We all know what kind of criticism Dan Brown has gone through. Ironically, the tremendous controversy over his book has made him a very wealthy man. I hadn't heard of *Three Marys*, nor have I read it, but it purportedly has gotten some acclaim and it just goes to show that no matter what kind of obstacles seem to be in the way, the truth about Jesus and Magdalene seems to be starting to rear its head. Although both of these books are fiction, they both leave readers to make their own conclusions, and certainly pique their interest to want to learn more.

Although Magdalene lived the last twenty years or so of her life in a cave, it was fairly comfortable. If the winter was unbearably harsh, she would go back to her house for the needed heat and comfort. For the most part, however, she remained in her cave, which seemed to her to be more private. Every morning Sarah would bring water up from a nearby well and would help Magdalene wash and get dressed. Magdalene and Sarah would then do their house-keeping, have breakfast, and many times a few friends would drop by. Magdalene would talk over breakfast about what visions she had and what her teachings for that day would be. Sarah would then help her out to the front of the cave, where people had gathered for her morning sermon. By this time Magdalene was very old and she had outlived all who were close to her except for Sarah. Jesus and Mary and Joseph of Arimathaea were all gone, and even though she had her followers, it was not like having the support system that had been around her for most of her life. She remarked to Sarah that she'd never believed she would live this long and outlive all the people who were dear to her. Even though she knew she had to stay to finish up what Jesus had started, it was bittersweet. She would pat Sarah's hand and then their day of teaching would begin.

She used Jesus's words from her visions, not only to console the populace, but also to console herself. She knew her visions were true because even though she was in a somewhat meditative state when she received them, Jesus would appear to her in full body form with a brilliant light behind him. He would also encourage her and tell her that time was fleeting and soon they would be together. At times she would also see Mary in her dreams, and she would lovingly tell Magdalene to have courage and patience and that her work, even though not quite finished, was the "pillar" by which Jesus's work would someday be recognized for what it really meant. Mary also told her that even if it took many years, the truth would win out.

Magdalene lived long enough to hear and even be privy to the infighting and the politics of power that surrounded Jesus and the early Church, and who was speaking truth and who was not. In her visions, Jesus would often tell her to keep her eyes on the goals they set, to turn a blind eye to what was happening in the Church, and to just keep preaching his words.

It's hard to hear and feel controversy surrounding someone you love. It is even harder to be the target or focal point of jealous and greedy men in their quest for power after your loved one is gone. It reminds me of siblings fighting over an inheritance. I feel this was many times harder because money is just money and is spent; but these pearls of wisdom that were simple and understandable were really an unobstructed road that would not only lead humankind to a better place in its soul but would also help people to deal with life and then go home.

When Magdalene was through with her day, Sarah and some of the women would have dinner waiting. They would have wine, bread soaked in olive oil, mutton, and wild berries. Then they would sit around a fire and talk about the day. When it was good weather, Magdalene would often go out with her writings to a nearby field where a large tree stood and go into meditation and prayer. Her head was completely covered now, and she wore long, flowing garments with a front piece like a scapular, making her look like a kind of nun.

Sometimes Magdalene would fall asleep under the tree. Sarah would come and get her, take her back to her cave, and lovingly put her to bed. Even though she was older now, her face was comparatively unlined and still glowed. She had kept her slender figure, but now she walked with a more faltering gait. Her unruly red hair that had been the bane of her life still was reddish but had a lot of gray, and she was glad that she could cover it. Every morning Sarah would either wash it or brush it with rose water, as Magdalene still had her unruly curls. The other ritual they did at least once a week was to wash each other's feet to show humility and to help their egos to stay static. They still celebrated Passover and the other Judaic holidays. When Magdalene's boys came of age, they had bar mitz-vahs to follow Judaic customs and traditions. Jesus had followed these customs when he was alive, and Magdalene just continued the tradition after he was gone.

Even though Sarah could begin to see a glowing light around her mother, she could also see a dimming of the light inside. It's like the feeling I get when I just know that someone is retracting from life. I saw it with all my loved ones and even with people I read for. Like I've said, germs and disease don't kill us—loss of purpose, grief, and people who are wrong for us make us sick enough to retract our life force.

Sometimes, in her reveries, Magdalene would go back in her memory to earlier times and almost relive bad parts like the crucifixion, but mostly she would relive the good times. She relived the times with Jesus and Mary and

Joseph, the talks, and especially the laughter that was always part of their lives. She even went back to her childhood and would see her and Jesus playing in the compound in Nazareth before he left on his journeys to the east, and these memories seemed as real to her as her present time did then. All time is in God's time, and the older we get the more we can truly see the circles within circles. Life begins to unfold like a multicolored montage.

Despite her advanced age, Magdalene pushed herself on, not only for the love of her husband and what he stood for, but for God and all those who she was told would come after. She knew that no matter how long it took, the truth would sustain the ages and come to the foreground of nonjudgmental Christianity. Other religions have had their wars and problems, but no religion has had as much infighting and as many factions and splits as Christianity. I suppose if humankind, unlike Peter, kept their egos out of it and quelled their quest for power and control, we all would just follow simple truths. We would no longer follow the statement "My God is better than your God." Magdalene certainly followed those simple truths and kept doing it.

Once in a while Sarah would chime in and team lecture with her mother, especially if Magdalene was getting overly tired, but this was fairly infrequent and she taught more after Magdalene's death. She only did it for a short time, however, because she died of a fever several months after her mother's death. This is probably why we don't hear much of Sarah or her bloodline—all the children of Jesus and Magdalene went their own way, and none but Sarah had any passion for the works of their mother and father. Francine says the bloodline died out within the next several hundred years because of pestilence and offspring dying from varying causes.

Much of the information that Magdalene received from Jesus has been lost to us, and we can only see glimpses of it in her gospel and in the Gospel of Thomas—which I love, because it has so many of Jesus's sayings in it. Francine says that some of this information will be found in future years, and all it can do is give greater insight into the divine messenger who we call Jesus.

Magdalene was now in her nineties, and she knew her time was nearing to meet her beloved family on the Other Side. She called the people together and told them her time had come and asked them to keep Jesus's words pure and to live the way he taught. There was an outpouring of grief among the people, but they knew she couldn't live forever and they could see her failing. Amazingly, as they had with Jesus before he died, some saw a golden light surrounding her.

She retired to her home attended by Sarah and a few women from the village. In large groups everyone kept vigil all night, praying and sobbing. She died very quietly, but just before she took her last breath she sat up with her eyes glowing and said, "Lord, I'm coming!" and then she was gone. When the gathered crowd heard that she was dead, there was a palpable silence, and then in almost complete unison they kneeled in prayer, knowing that she was finally home and her trials here were over.

Sarah planned a celebration. Not just for Magdalene, bur also for her grandmother and Jesus, to celebrate that they were finally together once again. They had completed a journey that many of us have taken, fraught with love, hate, ignorance, and sacrifice, and now there was a new beginning. It is called life. They had gone as far as they could, and it was their responsibility to give out the truth. It is our responsibility to unearth it again.

If any of you still say the prayer "Blessed Mary, Mother of God," you might just include Magdalene's name also ... because she truly was the first disciple and Jesus loved her the most.

God love you ... I do ...

Sylvia

A Note from Sylvia

As in *The Mystical Life of Jesus*, I find it important to honor more than one perspective on the Bible. *The Two Marys* cites the Bible using translations from both the King James and Douay-Rheims versions.

I am grateful for the use of the following works in *The Two Marys*. I thank the authors for their support.

"The Formation of the New Testament Canon" by Richard Carrier. http://www.infidels.org/library/modern/richard_carrier/NTcanon.html. Published with permission from The Secular Web, 2000.

The Gospel of Mary of Magdala: Jesus and the First Woman Apostle, by Karen L. King. Santa Rosa, CA: Polebridge Press, 2003. Used by permission.

The Tenets of Novus Spiritus

I   The way of all peace is to scale the mountain of self. Loving others makes the climb down easier. We see all things darkly until love lights the lamp of the soul.

II   Whatever thou lovest, lovest thou.

III   Do not give unto God any human pettiness such as vengeance, wrath, or hate. Negativity is man's alone.

IV   Create your own heaven, not a hell. You are a Creator made from God.

V Turn thy power outward, not inward, for therein shines the Light and the Way.

VI In faith be like the wind chimes. Hold steady until faith, like the wind, moves you to joy.

VII Know that each life is a path winding toward perfection. It is the step after step that is hard, not the whole of the journey.

VIII Be simple, allow no man to judge you, not even yourself, for you cannot judge God.

IX You are a Light in a lonely, dark desert that enlightens many.

X Let no one convince you that you are less than a God. Do not let fear imprison your spiritual growth.

XI Do not allow the unfounded belief in demons to block your communion with God.

XII The body is a living temple unto God, wherein we worship the spark of the Divine.

XIII   God does not create the adversities in life. By your own choice they exist to aid in your perfection.

XIV   Karma is nothing more than honing the wheel of evolvement. It is not retribution, but merely a balancing of experiences.

XV   God allows each person the opportunity for perfection, whether you need one life or a hundred lives to reach your level of perfection.

XVI   Devote your life, your soul, your very existence to the service of God. For only there will you find meaning in life.

XVII   War is profane; defense is compulsory. We support an individual's choice to be a conscientious objector.

XVIII Death is the act of returning home; it should be done with grace and dignity. You may preserve that dignity by refusing prolonged use of artificial life support systems. Let God's will be done.

XIX We believe in a Mother God, who is a co-creator to our all-loving Father.

XX We believe that our Lord was crucified, but did not die on the cross and went on to live His Life in France with His mother and Mary Magdalene, His wife.

XXI We the Gnostics kept the knowledge hidden that Christ's lineage exists even today, and the truth, long buried, is open to research.

XXII We absolutely reject the Book of Revelation and the Apocalypse.

Sylvia Browne is the #1 *New York Times* bestselling author of *Psychic Children; The Mystical Life of Jesus; Insight; Phenomenon; Prophecy; Visits from the Afterlife; The Other Side and Back; Past Lives; Future Healing;* and *Adventures of a Psychic.* She has been working as a psychic for five decades and appears regularly on *The Montel Williams Show.* She has also appeared on *Larry King Live, Good Morning America,* CNN, and *Entertainment Tonight.* Visit her Web site at www.sylvia.org. She lives in California.